ALOVEDLIFE

AN ABSOLUTE LOVE PUBLISHING SPECIAL EDITION
VOLUME 3

When you are clear, you can experience more of the love that is who you truly are. With your increasing radiance you become a beacon of light to an ever-widening circle.
~ *Personal Power through Awareness*

CONSCIOUSLY CREATE A LIFE YOU LOVE

Almost a
HUNDRED
contributors

DOZENS
of publications

ONE MISSION:

to create and publish projects promoting goodness in the world

ABSOLUTE LOVE PUBLISHING
www.absolutelovepublishing.com

ALOVEDLIFE

A PUBLICATION OF
ABSOLUTE LOVE PUBLISHING

Intentional Living

Elevated Action

Conscious Connection

Sacred Self-Care

Plus:

Publisher
Caroline A. Shearer

Editor
Sarah Hackley

Ambassador
Denise Thompson

Cover Photo by Nastya Gepp

LOVE ALOVEDLIFE?

Welcome to the third edition of ALOVEDLIFE, a book-magazine hybrid designed to help you consciously create a life you love. With evergreen content on Intentional Living, Elevated Action, Conscious Connection, and Sacred Self-Care, the tools and wisdom in ALOVEDLIFE will uplift and enhance your life so you can be your happiest and most fulfilled.

And we are **just getting started**! Find additional ALOVEDLIFE editions, pre-order options (so you always have the latest content), and much more (including our selection of books and min-e-books™) in our online store: www.absolutelovepublishing.com/shop.

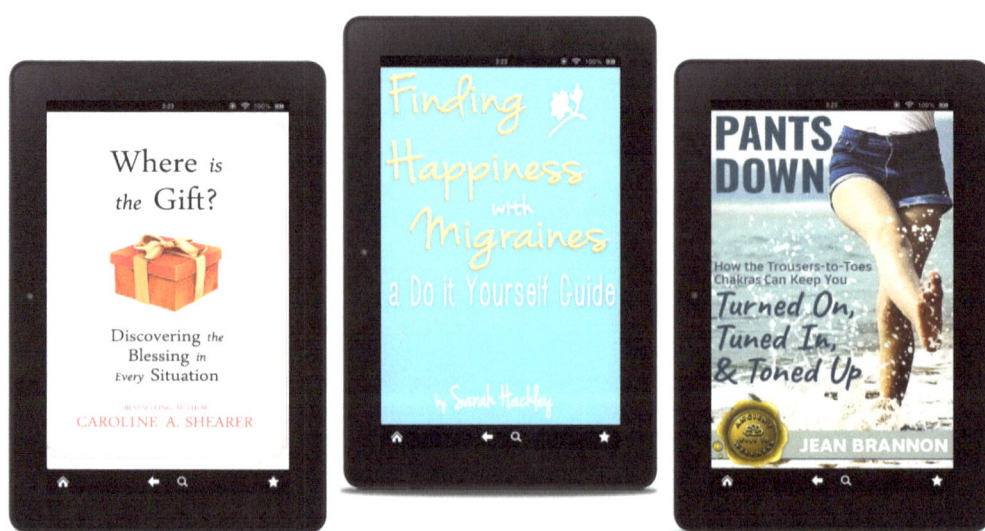

Set your life on fire. Seek those who fan your flames.

_____

Run from what's comfortable. Forget safety. Live where you fear to live. Destroy your reputation. Be notorious. I have tried prudent planning long enough. From now on I'll be mad.

- RUMI

I don't want a safe space. I want people who will bump and push up against me and make me better. Challenge me. Light a fire. Call me out when I've gone too far or not gone far enough.

Safe spaces leave us no reason to challenge ourselves, no reason to question, no reason to grow. They enable us to fall back into our imaginary boundaries and stay huddled alongside the insecurities and fears and pains that we coddle and indulge when "safe".

Instead, let's bump and bang against each other during this existence. Let's appreciate that the only real safety in this life is our sense of self, and to grow that we must inherently be "unsafe".

Let's free ourselves from self-created confines and open ourselves up to the magnificent expanse that is waiting for us – that freedom and light – that lies just beyond where we feel safe.

Let's let life polish us because while each of us is a beautiful, lustrous soul, it is that varied and jumbled path of the human experience that allows us to appreciate just how exquisite we truly are.

- Caroline A. Shearer

In 2012, I wrote this article for *Law of Attraction* magazine. At the time, I was in awe of all that had happened since the creation of my publishing house, Absolute Love Publishing.

I'm a big believer in serving our "highest and greatest" purpose, no matter how big or small that purpose might seem at different times of our lives. By following this path, I believe we are in harmony with our destiny, while also experiencing the greatest amount of personal fulfilment. But — I've found it takes bravery, grit, and determination on a daily basis to make and stick to the choices that are most in alignment with our true selves. That can feel tough sometimes, for sure. Maybe even a little impossible. Those struggles, though, have provided resistance that has made me even stronger in my beliefs and my direction.

There have been new challenges since writing this article, but I continue to work and create in ways that I love, now with even more published books and authors. I'd say it's more than I could have dreamed, but that wouldn't be true: I dreamed every bit of it into life. And, for whatever your dreams are, so can you.

Real-Life Success Story:

Synchronicities Showed the Way

The Universe brought together all the right people — and circumstances — to help me create a book about unconditional love

Caroline A. Shearer

A couple of years ago, I sat at my computer, surrounded by positive messages, crystals, and vision boards, hoping for the best. After praying to discover the "highest and best use" of my natural talents, I'd had an idea for a book: I wanted to explore the concept of love without conditions. Specifically, I wanted to share other people's stories of how they had learned to release conditions on love.

At the time, there were many unknowns: How would I find people who had stories to share? Would anyone even understand what I was looking for? And, would readers be ready to explore this topic?

This book project was a daring undertaking for me. I had just founded a new publishing company with the intention of creating and promoting goodness in the world, and I wanted to utilize my experience with the written word to make change on my own terms. My new direction was completely uncharted.

Despite diving into the unknown, I never experienced fear. I may have wondered how it would all happen, but somehow, deep inside, I knew it would. And, I realized very quickly that my intention to share this concept of unconditional love was supported by the universe. As soon as I set foot on this path, incredible individuals appeared. It was one surprise after another, until it felt like it was raining

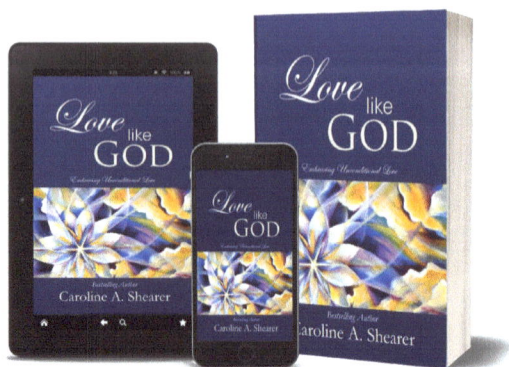

blessings every day!

Internationally-acclaimed musician Deva Premal, known for her beautiful rendition of the Gayatri Mantra, said she would like to share her journey of learning to love herself. An amazing woman and spiritually-inclined publicist named Dea Shandera contacted me seemingly out of the blue through our website to let me know she could deliver well-known individuals for the project. And, deliver she did! Through those connections, Mark Victor Hansen, co-founder of the Chicken Soup for the Soul series, endorsed the book, and his now-wife author Crystal Dwyer also shared her own story.

As the days and weeks went on, even more wonderful people appeared in my "inbox" – international models, bestselling authors, and esteemed professionals. Wonderful influencers took it upon themselves to tell media outlets and their connections about it. I received assistance among professionals for the actual work, such as editorial and graphics support. It was an affirming experience.

But — before this sounds like too "perfect" of a manifestation, let me tell you the rest of the story ...

There was a time when the book, eventually named *Love Like God,* felt like the *only* thing going

> Personal challenges popped up left and right, until I literally laughed out loud in exasperation: How many things could the Universe send me to deal with at once?
> (The answer is *a lot!*)

right in my world. I was incredibly happy to be working on it, but in others' views, I was doing it at my own detriment. Financial stress gnawed away at me, try as I did to release it. Personal challenges popped

---

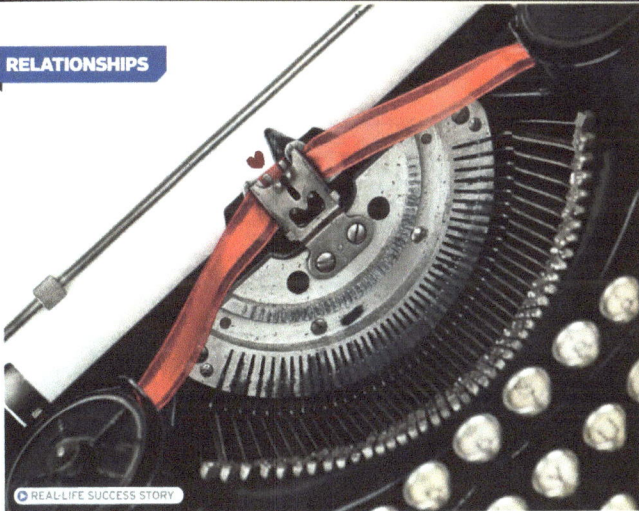

● REAL-LIFE SUCCESS STORY

Synchronicities Showed the Way

THE UNIVERSE BROUGHT TOGETHER ALL THE RIGHT PEOPLE—AND CIRCUMSTANCES—TO HELP ME CREATE A BOOK ABOUT UNCONDITIONAL LOVE

BY CAROLINE A. SHEARER

▶ **A COUPLE OF YEARS AGO,** I sat at my computer, surrounded by positive messages, crystals, and vision boards, hoping for the best. After praying to discover the "highest and best use" of my natural talents, I had an idea for a book: I wanted to explore the concept of love without conditions. Specifically, I wanted to share other people's stories of how they had learned to release conditions on love.

At the time, there were many unknowns: How would I find people who had stories to share? Would anyone even understand what I was looking for? And would readers be ready to explore this topic?

This book project was a daring undertaking for me. I had just founded a new publishing company with the intention of creating and promoting goodness in the world, and I wanted to utilize my experience with the written word to make change on my own terms. My new direction was completely uncharted.

Despite diving into the unknown, I never experienced fear. I may have wondered *how* it would all happen, but somehow, deep inside, I knew it would. And I realized very quickly that my intention to share this concept of unconditional love was supported by the Universe. As soon as I set foot on this path, incredible individuals appeared. It was one surprise after another, until it felt like it was raining blessings every day!

Internationally acclaimed musician Deva Premal, known for her beautiful rendition of the Gayatri Mantra, said she would like to share her journey of learning to love herself. An amazing woman and spiritually inclined publicist named Dea Shandera contacted me seemingly out of the blue through our website to let me know she could deliver well-known individuals for the project, and deliver she did! Through those connections, Mark Victor Hansen, cofounder of the *Chicken Soup for the Soul* series, endorsed the book, and his now-wife, author Crystal Dwyer, also shared her own story.

As the days and weeks went on, even more wonderful people appeared in my "inbox"—international models, bestselling authors, and esteemed professionals. Wonderful influencers took it upon themselves to tell media outlets and their connections about my book. I received assistance from professionals for the actual work, such as editorial and graphics support. It was an affirming experience.

But, before this sounds like too "perfect" a manifestation, let me tell you the rest of the story.

There was a time when the book, eventually named *Love Like God,* felt like the *only* thing going right in my world. I was incredibly happy to be working on it, but in others' views, I was doing it to my own detriment. Financial stress gnawed away at me, try as I did to release it. Personal challenges popped up left and right, until I literally laughed out loud in exasperation: How many things could the Universe send me to deal with at once? (The answer is *a lot!*)

Over and over, I reminded myself, "This is the time most people give up."

This movement toward what I view as my larger life purpose was an interesting juxtaposition. Everything and everyone involved in the book was fantastic. People I knew in other ways, however, said, "I support you . . . but."

Let's just say, I had enough "buts" in my head already! I wanted to hear, "I support you, and *here's why.*" I believe in unconditional support — absolute support, if you will — and it would have felt nourishing to be reminded of why I *could* create this book, why my particular qualities *would* help me achieve my mission.

At the time, I did my best to appreciate the "buts" for being what people had within them to offer, and then I did my best to fulfill my own craving for the "here's why." I wasn't hearing what I wanted from others, yet I was hearing what I needed, because it made me even more determined.

I found myself in the "muddle" of a transformation that felt sticky, messy, and downright painful. But, as uncomfortable as it was, I believe my higher self was helping me transition out of environments and relationships and mind-sets that wouldn't work with the even bigger version of myself I was creating. And, as synchronicity would have it, it was excellent practice for me to further explore the concept of absolute love. It challenged me to continue to love others, and it also reminded me to continue to love myself, no matter what. Ultimately, loving myself through these encounters planted me even further into a mind-set and heart-set of unconditional love.

While sometimes it felt like I was going backward, downward, or sideways, I was gaining remarkable skills. Those times trained me to be incredibly resourceful. They honed my determination even further. And, perhaps most important, they showed the door to those who weren't meant to be a part of my life *and* opened the door to those who were.

Ultimately, the experience shifted my understanding of the Law of Attraction. I realized: *There is a certain level of trust we have to turn over to our souls.*

Yes, we do the work. We say the affirmations. We improve our emotions and thoughts. We imagine ourselves as magnetic to all that is good.

But, the truth is, we're ready when we're ready, and we have to trust that wherever or however we are at any time is how we are meant to be in that moment.

Today, I am continuing my mission of creating goodness in the world through the written word. Those who offered me conditional support fell out of my life. Those who said "here's why" remain.

My latest book, *Women Will Save the World,* is filled with stories from Olympians, *Billboard*-topping musicians, visionary media professionals, authors, and other remarkable women. The right people continue to appear at the right moments, and it feels absolutely natural and absolutely incredible at the same time. The people I attract tend to want to help me and my mission. That simple fact continues to amaze and delight me, and perhaps this is why I continue to attract these people—and these amazing synchronicities—in abundance.

With love, Caroline

Bestselling author **Caroline A. Shearer** is the founder of Absolute Love Publishing and its imprint, Spirited Press (AbsoluteLove Publishing.com). Her popular books include *Dead End Date,* the first book in the Adventures of a Lightworker metaphysical mystery series; *Love Like God: Embracing Unconditional Love; Love Like God Companion Book; Raise Your Vibration: Tips and Tools for a High-Frequency Life,* a mini-e-book™; and *Women Will Save the World.*

up left and right, until I literally laughed out loud in exasperation: How many things could the Universe send me to deal with at once? (The answer is *a lot!*)

Over and over, I reminded myself, "This is the time most people give up."

This movement toward what I view as my larger life purpose was an interesting juxtaposition. Everything and everyone involved in the book was fantastic. People I knew in other ways, however, said, "I support you ... but."

Let's just say, I had enough "buts" in my head already! I wanted to hear, "I support you, and *here's why*". I believe in unconditional support – absolute support, if you will – and it would have felt nourishing to be reminded of why I *could* create this book, why my particular qualities *would* help me achieve my mission.

At the time, I did my best to appreciate the "buts" for being what people had within them to offer, and then I did my best to fulfill my own craving for the "here's why". I wasn't hearing what I wanted from others, yet I was hearing what I needed, because it made me even more determined.

I found myself in the "muddle" of a transformation that felt sticky, messy, and downright painful. But, as uncomfortable as it was, I believe my higher self was helping me transition out of environments and relationships and mindsets that wouldn't work with the even bigger version of myself that I was creating. And, as synchronicity would have it, it was excellent practice for me to further explore the concept of absolute love. It challenged me to continue to love others, and it also reminded me to continue to love myself, no matter what. Ultimately, loving myself through these encounters planted me even

further into a mindset and heart-set of unconditional love.

While sometimes it felt like I was going backwards, downwards, or sideways, I was gaining remarkable skills. Those times trained me to be incredibly resourceful. They honed my determination even further. And, perhaps most importantly, they showed the door to those who weren't meant to be a part of my life *and* opened the door to those who were.

Ultimately, the experience shifted my understanding of the Law of Attraction. I realized: *There is a certain level of trust we have to turn over to our souls.*

Yes, we do the work. We say the affirmations. We improve our emotions and thoughts. We imagine ourselves as magnetic to all that is good.

But, the truth is, we're ready when we're ready, and we have to trust that wherever or however we are at any time is how we are meant to be in that moment.

But, the truth is, we're ready when we're ready, and we have to trust that wherever or however we are at any time is how we are meant to be in that moment.

Today, I am continuing my mission of creating goodness in the world through the written word. Those who offered me conditional support fell out of my life. Those who said "here's why" remain.

Ultimately, the experience shifted my understanding of the Law of Attraction. I realized: *There is a certain level of trust we have to turn over to our souls.*

CHAKRA STAIRCASE MEDITATION

Download at
www.AbsoluteLovePublishing.com

CALL FOR

SOCK IT TO 'EM
SOCK AMBASSADORS

As a Sock It to 'Em Sock Campaign Sock Ambassador, you will organize sock collections in your own city as part of the overall Sock It to 'Em Sock Campaign. Collected socks are distributed to organizations in your area that support children, women's shelters, and those experiencing homelessness.

Volunteer to fit your schedule, and see firsthand the local impact of your work!

START YOUR SOCK CAMPAIGN TODAY!

SOCKITTOEMSOCKCAMPAIGN.ORG/BECOME-AN-AMBASSADOR/

FIND YOUR TIGER

Lisa Capri

Four-letter words get a bad reputation. You know the ones I mean. They're rarely used while in positive flow and their contribution to our well-being is questionable.

But there's ONE four-letter word that has chameleon-like powers to move from a negative energetic flow to a positive one.

This word is so powerful that it can debilitate or motivate.

It can stifle your deepest desires or unleash your true power.

It can bring you to your knees or it can propel you toward your goals at lightning speed.

Have you guessed what it is?

It's FEAR.

We've all seen the memes on social media. F.E.A.R. for "forget everything and run" (a nod to our neurological fight-or-flight reaction) is contrasted against "face everything and rise".

It's all in the interpretation, isn't it?

Conventionally, fear is a simple, basic emotion. But it operates far beyond a basic emotion. It can *be* and *do* so much more than you might realize.

Popular personal-development literature will tell you that in order to truly grow and achieve your wildest goals, you have to do something that scares you every day. The result of letting fear into your life and your everyday consciousness, however, can have either negative or positive consequences. It all depends on what you *do* with the fear.

You can allow it to dim your light on this planet, or you can allow it to light your path.

The way to make fear result in positive consequences is to bring it forward purposefully and intentionally — to really lean into that fear.

Can we sit with our fear for a few minutes a day? We sure can. We already do this when we question our abilities, when we look at life from a mindset of lack (personal or professional), or when we worry about something that hasn't happened yet. But that's sitting with our fear in a way that doesn't serve us. We also can choose to sit in our fear in a way that *does*.

There's a fundamental difference between letting fear through the door uninvited versus calling upon fear intentionally to serve a higher purpose. It's this strange paradoxical scenario that I'd like to unpack here. Hopefully, it will inspire you to invite fear into your life with purpose and intention.

The Desire to Level Up

Anytime I have ever wanted to level up in my personal or professional life and I began to take action to support a particular goal, I noticed a pattern emerge. Obstacles were thrown in my path. No matter what my goal was, something unfortunate always happened that stopped me in my tracks and forced me to temporarily scale back the efforts I had been making. Or worse, it caused me to question the validity or viability of the goal I'd been seeking to achieve.

As an example, if I decide that I'd like to lose 20 pounds and begin a new exercise and nutrition program tomorrow, chances are good that I will fall ill or sustain a minor injury shortly after beginning. Based on similar experiences in the past, this will inevitably cause me to take a small break from my efforts. This happens to me all the time.

As another example, imagine that I set a goal to grow my audience by 500 email subscribers in the next 30 days. I take a workshop to learn tactics and strategies related to this goal. I begin to take some of the action necessary to support the goal, and I start gaining some traction. Then … whack! I'm hit with some new or recurring obstacle that throws me off my chosen path and sets me back several days, weeks, or even months. My momentum is lost.

In both scenarios, I set a specific goal that was

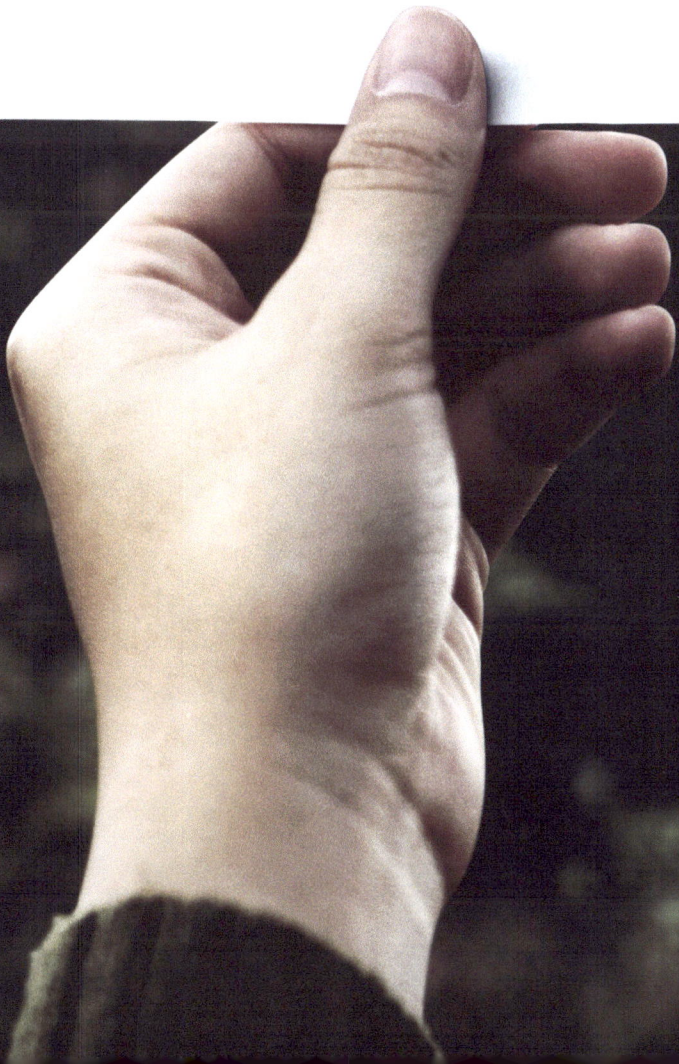

measurable and attainable, I knew which actions to take to support the goal, and I had even begun taking consistent action. In other words, I was doing all the things the personal-development books were saying I should be doing.

So why did the inevitable obstacles keep coming, and why did they derail me?

If something similar has ever happened to you, you might have chalked it up to "bad luck". If that "bad luck" has happened enough to establish a pattern, you might have begun to think that you're just not destined to be fit or that you're meant to be stuck in one place professionally. Sometime later, back at square one, you might decide to start over. But, you also might throw your hands up in the air and think you're just not cut out for that kind of success.

That's simply not true.

I believe that these obstacles happen to test our will and our grit. More importantly, I believe, they teach us to push through and be creative thinkers. The *problem* is that we often never make it through these tests because of our misunderstood relationship with fear.

Fear is Just an Ingredient

Deep-seated feelings of not being good enough and of not deserving success are just fear in disguise, but they're not the good kind of fear.

This is why we're able to get to the point of making the New Year's resolution to lose weight or to change our professional or financial situation. This is why we're able to start taking consistent action. But somewhere down the road, an obstacle presents itself and we abandon the path.

We might justify it by saying someone or something else needs our attention more than our goals. But most of us will chalk this up to our own lack of motivation or discipline. In other words, we start to think something is wrong with *us*. But this couldn't be further from the truth.

Motivation and discipline are just two of the ingredients needed to move the needle forward.

The third ingredient is FEAR.

The Sliding Scale

Motivation, discipline, and fear live on a sliding scale. We first become motivated to make a change typically for a superficial (external) reason. We want to lose 20 pounds to look better in our clothes. We want to level up our career to have more money. Fair enough.

Given enough time on the right path, we then slide into discipline, which is *very* different from motivation. Discipline is a muscle we develop over time so that when our motivation is lacking on a given day, we can rely on our discipline to support us and see us through.

But when the going gets tough, our motivation and discipline are not enough. We need fear to get us to the finish line.

Traditionally seen as a negative motivator, fear also can play the role of a positive force in your life — if you know how to leverage it. It's all in how you construct your idea of fear.

Historically, our fight-or-flight fear instinct developed based on our need for survival. A giant tiger was chasing you? Your adrenaline kicked in to either help you fight the animal or run faster than you'd ever run before just to escape.

In today's modern world, our day-to-day "survival" is more about strengthening our mindset than about outrunning predators. Since there are no tigers chasing us as we go about our daily tasks, we need to simulate a type of fear that can keep us on course. If we don't, we risk falling into a habitual pattern of giving up or feeling inadequate.

Find Your Tiger

If an actual tiger were chasing you, you wouldn't stop to ponder whether you could outrun him, whether your mother-in-law would approve, or whether your outfit would make your figure look stocky as you ran for your life (or stayed to fight). You would just react.

What if we brought that same type of reaction time to any big challenge or new goal that's out of our comfort zone? What if we made it a point to skip the self-doubt?

I'm not suggesting we make all of our important life decisions on impulse, but rather that we use our old biological programming to get us moving in the right direction, even if it's only a small step forward. (Get off the couch and lace up your shoes. Book the appointment to dye your hair purple if you've always dreamed of a funky hair color. Ask for that raise at work.)

What I *am* suggesting is that you find your tiger by going deeper into your thought process. What are you *really* afraid of if you don't achieve your goal? Go deeper than the surface-level motivation.

The 20 pounds you want to lose is not really about looking better in your clothes. It's about what will happen if you *don't* lose the 20 pounds. Use your power of imagination to stir up some fear about what the next 10 years will look like if you don't get a handle on your health now. What's the worst scenario you can think of that truly scares you? Not being able to chase your children around the yard because of your weight? The pain in your joints from additional pressure? Obesity-related heart failure?

The higher-earning potential you seek isn't just

You can allow fear
to dim your light
on this planet, or
you can allow it
to light your path.

about having more money in your bank account or status in your community. It's what you're afraid will happen if you don't ask for the raise, go for the promotion, or start that dream business on the side. What's the scariest, plausible situation you can imagine? Not having the funds to send your child to college? Bouncing your mortgage payments? Not having the funds to take the family vacations you desperately want to emulate from your youth?

Find *your* tiger – the one that really scares you. This tiger will look different to everyone. It's *your* tiger, and it's coming for you.

You can now react by taking the action required to help you achieve your goal.

Remember that sliding scale?

Here's where it gets interesting. If you begin with your *true*, deeper fear in mind (what happens if you don't succeed), you start off with better (intentional and defined) motivation, which builds better (purposeful) discipline.

On the days when your motivation wavers, both your true fear (which you can visualize vividly) and your better-quality discipline will be there to back you up.

Personalize Your Fear

I encourage you to come up with your own acronym for the word fear or borrow one or two of mine.

If you find your tiger, **F**ear **E**vokes **A**wesome **R**esults.

If you find your tiger, **F**ear **E**ngages **A**mazing **R**esults.

Once you learn to use your fear purposefully and intentionally, you turn the negative charge of fear (producing your adrenaline) into a positive charge that amps up your motivation. Your motivation then drives your exercise of discipline, and you continue to take the action(s) needed to achieve your goal.

Obstacles are inevitable, but failure isn't.

Fear is optional, but I highly recommend it.

During the process of writing this article, I feared it wouldn't be good enough. I had a few obstacles thrown in my path along the way, too (illness, unexpected personal issues, etc.). But it was only when I dug into my true fear about not completing the article that it finally got done.

Deep down, my fear was about not following through on a commitment that meant so much to me.

Even deeper down was the fear that if I didn't write this article, someone who really needed to read these words wouldn't have them to light *their* path.

I dug even deeper, and while sitting in my fear, I had visions of a woman who needed the courage to leave a toxic relationship.

Then of a woman who needed the courage to ask for help when she needed it, irrespective of what others thought.

Then of a woman who desperately needed to find a way to finance her dream business, no matter how impossible it seemed at that moment.

And while sitting in that fear, I realized that I *am* each of those women.

I found *my* tiger. And she's the version of myself that doesn't act in alignment with her true desires. Like an evil twin running toward me with every scary weapon imaginable.

I can defeat her because I can lean into my fear and use it as rocket fuel to propel me forward.

I found my tiger.

Have *you*?

Find your tiger – the one that really scares you. This tiger will look different to everyone. It's *your* tiger, and it's coming for you.

Lisa Capri has owned and operated businesses in various fields for more than 15 years. She is the host of the *Raise Your Frequency Podcast*, a weekly show that tackles productivity and lifestyle habits for entrepreneurs. Lisa is obsessed with creating systems to get laser-focused on business goals while continuing to grow in one's personal life. Visit her at lisacapri.com.

BUSY or HAPPY

Making a Conscious Choice

SARAH HACKLEY

Imagine you have a free day. Your partner, if you have one, is on a work trip or otherwise completely occupied for the next 24 hours. Your kids, if you have them, are with grandparents or friends for the day and night. There's no one to feed, bathe, clothe, or put first. There's no work hanging over your head and no appointments to attend. You're completely free.

What do you do?

Most of us in this scenario picture ourselves doing something we love or engaging in our preferred method(s) of self-care. Maybe we picture ourselves finally getting around to that book we've been aching to read or movie we've been waiting to see. Maybe we envision ourselves getting lost in our favorite hobby or relaxing wherever we feel most at peace. Maybe we see ourselves taking a hot bath, a restful nap, or a long walk. Whatever it is we picture ourselves doing, it is almost always something relaxing, stress-free, joyful — and far from what we actually end up doing when we finally get that free time.

Instead, when we do get those precious, unscheduled moments, we fill them with busywork. We catch up on housework and laundry. We pay bills and manage our budgets. We wash our cars, meal prep, and scratch off a few other items on our never-ending list of to-dos. Often, we even convince ourselves that this is a better use of our time.

That is a problem.

Relaxation and idleness are integral to the human experience. Unscheduled, unrushed time to do what we most enjoy doing fosters creativity, reduces stress, and promotes wellbeing. It also bolsters happiness.

Happiness has numerous causes (physical, physiological, mental, and emotional) and can manifest in many ways, but the why and how aren't always as important as the when. Because the when matters. Those idle moments matter. Actively engaging in idleness helps us to see life for the explorative journey it is. And it is in that journey that we find our joy. If, instead, we see life only as a means to an end, we deny ourselves the happiness that comes from those moments.

Unfortunately, prioritizing relaxation is almost revolutionary in today's busy-oriented world. Happiness itself is seen as a thing we have to strive for — a thing to do, something to chase. In reality, happiness comes in part by allowing ourselves the space to just be.

To grant ourselves that space, however, we must cast off the often-ingrained belief that busyness and productivity are what creates worth and value. We also have to let go of the guilt or shame we may feel when we are decidedly un-busy. These emotional weights stop us from fully experiencing the "unproductive" moments that nurture our wellbeing and create happiness.

We can overcome these roadblocks by choosing to prioritize free time and, like any new skill, practice it until it feels comfortable.

How to Prioritize Free-Time

At least once a week, block out a chunk of time on your calendar as unscheduled free time — as in, a block of time with absolutely no expectations on it. When that time comes around, resist the urge to fill it with busy work or to go on an errand. Instead, give yourself the space to breathe in the full, present moment.

When the time comes, ask yourself what would feel most relaxing in that moment, and then give yourself permission to do that.

It sounds so simple, and yet … It might feel foreign. It might feel difficult.

You may feel the urge to check your email or clean the kitchen. Your mind might circle what you feel

you "should" be doing — those pesky little to-dos on your never-ending list or even some project you've been "meaning to get to".

Why should I read this novel when I could get a head start on dinner? How can I take a bath when I need to go buy that item for my child's school project? Just that one check of social media …

Resist the urge to act on those things, even if it means you don't fully relax that first week or even that first month. Block out the time anyway, and exercise discipline in re-training yourself to let go.

As you practice letting yourself simply exist, it will get easier to relax into the moment. The urge to check your messages will dull. Your to-do list will fade into the background. And you will experience something that is all-too-rare in our lives: release.

When you reach that point, you will find you fully enjoy your moments of rest and are completely comfortable letting go of other demands. When that happens, applaud yourself! And then, relax some more.

Flip the Script

These moments can equal more than just taking a break. They can bring to life the parts of ourselves that so easily get lost in the rush and go-go-go of our everyday lives.

Often, we say we would like to have more relaxation time, but, again and again, we find excuses to skip it. Instead of viewing relaxation as time "missing out" on being productive, flip that mental script to what you will gain from a time-out. This might include renewed calmness, fresh approaches to challenges, and more joy in the day-to-day. These additions to your life are what can help you both appreciate your busy times and blossom in your free time.

And the next time you face a choice between being busy or being happy, may you choose to be happy.

Sarah Hackley is the editor for Absolute Love Publishing and the author of *Finding Happiness with Migraines: A Do It Yourself Guide, Preparing to Fly: Financial Freedom from Domestic Abuse,* and *The Things We Lose.* She also is a patient advocate, writing and wellness coach, and poet. Learn more at www.sarahhackley.com.

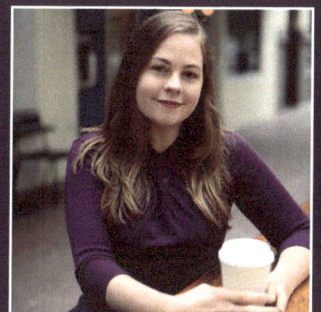

POWER UP YOUR LIFE

with RED, ORANGE, & YELLOW

JEAN RUDKO

If you spend much time with young children you're sure to be asked one of their most-loved questions: "What's your favorite color?" Though the question seems simple on its surface, kids understand that the response reveals something essential about the person answering. As adults, we tend to lose sight of this fact.

Colors are important, and how we choose to use them can have a profound effect on our emotional and physical wellbeing. While few people, if asked, would name beige or gray as a favorite color, countless closets, homes, and offices are filled with these dull neutral tones. Unfortunately, according to color theory, this may be having unintended negative consequences on those of us living and working in these spaces.

Our preferences for certain colors is deeply personal and how we respond may depend on the climate, our mood when viewing a color, gender, age, and our culture or memory associations. When we see a particular color, like gray or red, our bodies react by releasing specific hormones into our bloodstreams. In turn, these hormones activate particular organs and create reactions we can physically feel. And these reactions and feelings differ depending on the particular color viewed. A warm color like red, for instance, can make us feel energized, passionate, and confident. A dull, neutral color like gray, on the other hand, can make us feel indecisive, detached, or subdued.

So the next time you're shopping, consider

The color red represents the power we all have within ourselves to make our dreams become reality.

choosing an item rich in the warm shades of red, orange, or yellow instead of reaching for another gray or tan piece to add to your collection. These more vibrant shades are stimulating colors with active energies that can raise your vibration and help boost your emotional and physical health. They also can enhance and empower your chakras and your life in very specific ways.

WISDOM FROM RED:
I AM Empowered

The color red represents the power we all have within ourselves to make our dreams become reality. In Chinese culture, red is the color of abundance and wealth and is considered lucky. Thus we see many Eastern businesses decorated with red tones.

Red links with and stimulates the first chakra, which is referred to as the Root Chakra. The Root Chakra is located at the base of the spine, the pelvic floor, and the first three vertebrae. This chakra governs the lower spine, kidneys, feet, rectum, and immune system.

The Root Chakra also is the chakra responsible for the acquisition of our basic needs in life: food, water, shelter, financial and physical security, and freedom from fear and anxiety. Balancing the first chakra is essential because it creates our foundation and affects the balance and harmony of every other chakra in the body. When the Root Chakra is balanced with red, we feel grounded and safe, and we tend to worry less.

Exploring the Root Chakra and an imbalance of the color red can help many people understand why they are prone to specific health issues. Red energizes all organs and the five senses. It combats fatigue, lethargy, colds, pneumonia, bronchitis, and asthma (all indications of a compromised immune system and weak red energy). Other physical dysfunctions such as lower back pain, sciatica, and varicose veins also may be a result of a Root Chakra deficient in red.

The color red energizes the heart and blood circulation, and so it is excellent for anemia and blood-related conditions. It builds up the blood by causing hemoglobin to multiply, thus increasing energy and raising body temperature.

Red evokes a wider range of emotions than other colors and allows us to express ourselves with confidence, to overcome procrastination, and to accomplish goals. It stimulates independence, courage, willpower, ambition, determination, and assertiveness. Because it is associated with vitality and enthusiasm for life, it also helps when dealing with change. For those of us who often dwell on the past, the color red can help to root us in the present.

There also is a fun, playful, and exciting side to red. It is the color most associated with passionate love, tenderness, and romance. (Red roses and red hearts are classic symbols of romantic love.) In addition to evoking feelings of passion and excitement, the color red even can help us feel younger and more attractive.

HOW TO INCORPORATE RED

Use these fun, simple methods to infuse red energy into your surroundings and reap this color's benefits:

Paint your door a bright red to draw positive energy into your home. (In Feng Shui, a red front door means "welcome".) The same principle can work to activate a positive flow of money by using a red wallet.

Snuggle up on the couch with a red blanket whenever you are feeling chilly. Looking at the color red can make you feel warmer.

Wear red to stand out, grab the spotlight, or attract romance. A red coat, dress, necklace, or even underwear can make you feel empowered and give you confidence. Put pep in your step with a pair of bright red shoes or draw attention to your mouth and cause people to remember what you are saying with red lipstick.

Place a small red vase or pencil holder on your desk to aid with attentiveness and better catch grammar, punctuation, spelling, and other errors.

Small pops of red can energize and brighten a dingy space. Add red throw pillows, a bowl of red fruit, or a piece of red-dominant art to a dull room and notice your energy rise.

Fair warning: A little of this color goes a long way! Since red is such a powerful color, be aware that too much red can cause feelings of agitation or overexcitement. (Watch out for too much red in bedrooms, for example.) But what's "too much" red varies with location and purpose. For instance, while a lot of red in a kitchen may feel overwhelming, the same amount in a formal dining room may whet appetites and make people think you are a better cook!

WISDOM FROM ORANGE:
I AM Sociable.

Orange is a helpful, friendly color and makes life seem happier. It sparks sociability and brings out our inherent good nature while helping us to expand our interests and activities.

Orange is energetic. It spurs creativity and is where the seeds of inventions and original ideas are planted and nurtured. Orange boosts our confidence and helps show us our limitless potential.

Like red, orange is attention-getting but not as overpowering. It can provide a boost of energy if we are feeling fatigued or depressed. Orange also offers emotional strength in difficult times and assists in recovery from grief. We live in the power of now with orange.

Orange stimulates the second chakra, referred to as the Sacral Chakra. This chakra runs from the lower abdomen to the navel and governs our sexual organs, stomach, upper intestine, liver, gallbladder, kidneys, pancreas, spleen, and middle spine. This is why the color orange relates to our "gut reactions" or "gut instincts", as opposed to the physical reactions of red and the mental reactions of yellow.

Incorporating orange can help soothe an irritable bowel, relieve gas in the digestive system, strengthen the lungs and kidneys, alleviate muscle spasms in all parts of the body, decrease menstrual cramps, and assist breastfeeding by stimulating lactation. Orange can be used for specific conditions such as arthritis, gout, asthma, bronchitis and respiratory diseases, gallstones, kidney ailments, and hypothyroidism.

HOW TO INCORPORATE ORANGE

Encourage communication and social connection by incorporating orange accessories or an orange wall into a living room, den, or children's playroom. Diffusing orange essential oil in the room will enhance sociability even more!

Improve lung function and increase energy during your workouts by carrying an orange hand towel or using an orange exercise ball or bright orange yoga mat at the gym.

Bring the abundance and bounty of the fall harvest into your home or workplace by displaying decorative pumpkins.

Eat an orange a day to keep your hands and feet warm in the cooler weather.

Expand joy and strengthen feelings of happiness

> Orange is energetic. It spurs creativity and is where the seeds of inventions and original ideas are planted and nurtured.

by spending time appreciating the color of orange in nature. Take in a breathtaking sunrise or sunset or bask in the beauty of the autumn leaves.

WISDOM FROM YELLOW:
I AM Happy.

Yellow energy is like a ray of sunshine that warms your body with a glow of self-confidence. This sunny color helps you feel happy, optimistic, and cheerful. It is associated with laughter and a good sense of humor.

Yellow stimulates the third chakra, referred to as the Solar Plexus Chakra, which is two inches above the navel in the abdominal area. This location

Yellow energy is like a ray of sunshine that warms your body with a glow of self-confidence. This sunny color helps you feel happy, optimistic, and cheerful.

governs the upper digestive system: stomach, bowels, liver, gallbladder, pancreas, and spleen.

Except for diarrhea, all digestive problems such as indigestion, nausea, bloating, cramps, constipation, stomach ulcers, and celiac disease can be alleviated with the color yellow. It speeds up digestion and assimilation by stimulating gastric juices and can assist with weight loss. Yellow is the brightest color used in color light therapy and can help with liver diseases such as hepatitis and cirrhosis by stimulating and purifying the liver.

Yellow also can assist with kidney problems, lymphatic congestions, pancreatitis, and conditions such as hypoglycemia. Interestingly, worms and insects shy away from the color yellow so it can be used to destroy intestinal worms by driving them out of the body.

Add more yellow into your life if you want to become more flexible and spontaneous or increase your self-esteem, self-worth, and self-love. Yellow also helps you see yourself as "good enough" and aids with decision making and reducing procrastination. Would you like to be more able to speak up for yourself? To release and let go of negativity? Well, you can count on yellow to help you with that!

Use yellow to increase your short-term memory and to aid with mental concentration and focus and to overcome nervous exhaustion.

HOW TO INCORPORATE YELLOW

Increase happiness by adding a pop of yellow to a room by painting the inside of your bookshelves yellow or by decorating with a vase of yellow flowers or a bowl of lemons. Diffuse the scent of lemon to evoke even more uplifting feelings.

One of the most uplifting ways to incorporate red, orange, and yellow into your life is by spending time appreciating these colors in nature.

Use yellow in an entryway or on a front porch to provide a boost of optimism before you embark on your day or to lift your spirits as you come home after a long day.

Wear yellow whenever you need an added boost in intelligence or memory, such as when you need to finish a work project or score high on an exam.

Note of warning: Like any color, yellow should be used in moderation. Yellow tends to reflect a lot of light and can irritate eyes in large quantities. It also is the most fatiguing to the eye and can lead to eye strain.

INCORPORATING WARM COLORS

Color is a powerful tool. Introducing the powerful colors of red, orange, and yellow through apparel, environment, diet, and decor can improve our moods, behaviors, and physical and mental health. In turn, these warm-color energies can help us attract the things we wish to attract into our lives.

One of the most uplifting ways to incorporate red, orange, and yellow into your life is by spending time appreciating these colors in nature. Other powerful ways to infuse the warm-color energies of red, orange, and yellow into your day is by using colored crystals or color-therapy glasses, saying color affirmations, drinking solarized water (water energized with certain colors), and meditating on or visualizing certain colors. Use balance when incorporating the strong colors of red, orange and yellow into your days, and you will find you can improve many areas of your life. Hurray for red, orange, and yellow!

My name is Jean Rudko, and I help people raise their vibes and balance their chakras with my many different modalities, skills, and products that can be put to work for you. I am a color specialist who incorporates color light therapy sessions, color card readings, and Colour Energy™ products.

As mentioned, one of the most significant ways for you to make use of color is by adding color to your surroundings. I love helping people add color to their decor with my colorful paintings. Check out my website for all my wonderful color products and services at www.colorfulwellness.ca.

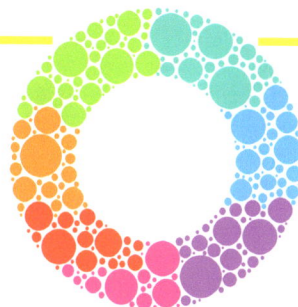

DEAR UNIVERSE:

My Life's Purpose Seems to Be Missing!

Karen Gruber Colp

As I approach another milestone birthday, I can't help but notice that I am surrounded by podcasts, life coaches, television interviews, social media posts, and self-help books all discussing how finding your life's purpose leads to inner peace, health, happiness, and pure joy.

Spiritual teachers and life coaches tell us that if our work is our life's purpose, it simply won't feel like work. Experts inform us that we will "just know" when we find what we were put on this earth to accomplish. It will be an undeniable feeling that we just can't mistake as anything but our personal mission. We will wake up each day with a sense of well-being and eagerness for the day ahead.

Well, if I'm being honest (and isn't that the point of sharing and writing and reading), the only feelings I woke up with this morning were indigestion from eating my son's cookies at 11 p.m. and a migraine from the noise level in my sixth-grade classroom. Frankly, I spend more mornings waking up to a sense of obligation than I do to a sense of inspiration. That doesn't mean I am ungrateful. In fact, just the opposite. I, too, have an abundance of gratitude journals listing my appreciation for my family and friends, as well as my appreciation for coffee and chocolate.

But, what I am talking about here is the inspiration of knowing what we are meant to be doing here on earth. The pure, unadulterated knowledge of our *Capital-P* Purpose. And, if there is one thing I do know for certain, it is that I have absolutely no idea what that Purpose is.

Growing up in a community of overachievers, I noticed that many friends and acquaintances knew at a young age exactly what they wanted to do when they grew up. Those few who didn't know had passionate interests. The child obsessed with animals became a vet or vet tech. The science-minded child became a pediatrician or cardiologist. The bookworm who scored a 1350 on her SAT's is now an avid writer or researcher. The straight-A valedictorian is out there saving the world with her Harvard law degree.

Then, there are those whose hobbies became their livelihoods: The talented artist who started a business painting murals for large corporations. The sensational musician who was waiting tables, writing and singing on off hours, until he got a big hit. The teens saving the world via remarkable non-profits. And then, of course, there are those who have taken their passions and reached almost unbelievable levels of fame and fortune using their gifts to contribute to the world like the entrepreneur with the million-dollar idea for a tech company.

As I learn more and more about this coveted "life purpose", I can't help but ask myself, "What in the world is wrong with me?" I mean, logically I know I

As I learn more and more about this coveted "life purpose", I can't help but ask myself, "What in the world is wrong with me?"

have value and that God put me here for a reason, and blah blah blah. But, all I can say for certain is that not knowing that reason but feeling like I *should* know just leads to an enormous amount of self-criticism and time wasted on introspection. And I know I'm not alone. There simply isn't any one thing that feels like *the* thing I am meant to be doing forever. But, I can't keep chasing my Purpose forever.

I mean, how many careers can one person have in a lifetime, really? I started in retail, but by the time the first customer asked me to find her shoe size in the stock room, I knew then and there that my role in the retail industry would go no further. I then spent 10 years in advertising, marketing, and public relations for the sole reason that it was my college major. And while it had its moments, being forced to

Maybe it's time for more journaling and self-reflection. Perhaps it's time again to take another life course, to quietly sneak to the self-help section of a distant bookstore in search of new tools to discover why I am here on this planet at this time.

---

choose a major at 17 didn't equate to a good life fit. Then, I had an idea. I wanted to teach!

I assumed that was it. Teaching must be the career I was meant to have. Kids love me, I love kids, and I am a nurturer. It had to be my Purpose! Twenty years later, I can tell you that, while I love it, there aren't many jobs harder than having 30, 11-year-old children pulling at you for every need under the sun for eight solid hours.

Is this the purpose God intended for me? To live life working a grueling, exhausting job that I both love and can't wait to escape at the end of each school year? Surely, there's more.

I tell myself I must have a calling.

Maybe it's time for more journaling and self-reflection. Perhaps it's time again to take another life course, to quietly sneak to the self-help section of a distant bookstore in search of new tools to discover why I am here on this planet at this time. Maybe it is time again to browse for tips on digging within and listening to my inner voice.

But as I ponder my next step, all my inner voice is telling me is that it is time for a double-shot latte.

As I take my first sip, I open the fridge and look around my kitchen. I see home. I see peace. I see a healthy dinner that I made from scratch waiting to be enjoyed by my son, my husband, and my parents. And I see all of the things I do daily that I truly enjoy — the various, random things that make a life for those of us who like to dabble in many things.

Which begs the question: In a time when we are supposed to focus on being in the present moment,

---

In a time when we are supposed to focus on being in the present moment, are there some of us who are meant to "just be"?

> If you're thinking you have to soul search for that one thing you were meant to do to hold your place in this world, and the only thing it is doing to you is crushing your soul, maybe it is time to let go of that limiting belief.

are there some of us who are meant to "just be"?

As I ponder, my brother calls and asks if I can watch the kids for an hour. A text comes in from my in-laws asking how my day was. An email arrives from my boss asking how a student in my class is doing. A friend texts asking me to give her son a ride to school tomorrow. And my son (at the last hour, of course) says he needs supplies for a school project.

It hits me. This normal, everyday life is it. I *can* just "be". *That* is my purpose.

So, if you're thinking you have to soul search for that one thing you were meant to do to hold your place in this world, and the only thing it is doing to you is crushing your soul, maybe it is time to let go of that limiting belief. As the gurus say, it just doesn't serve you anymore!

There are those who know they have a calling, a passion, to contribute to the world. And there are those, like me, who contribute in small, simple ways by simply being present in the small moments of everyday life. And both are okay.

As my husband reminds me, we need all kinds of people in this world. We can't all be the same. There are those who are meant to fly, and there are those, like the song goes, who are the wind beneath their wings. And that is a purpose I can live with.

Karen Gruber Colp has been on a spiritual journey seeking answers to life's toughest questions for as long as she can recall. She earned a University of Florida Journalism and Communications degree and a Master of Business Administration from Nova Southeastern University. She worked in Advertising, Marketing, and PR before accepting a teaching job that included designing a writing workshop enabling all children to enjoy the art of creative writing. A teacher for over 20 years, she resides in Hollywood, Florida, and her family includes a husband, son, two dogs, and a cat.

Quieting Our Minds

One of the biggest challenges most of us face in striving to live a high-vibration life is quieting our minds. And, it's no wonder, given how most meditation is portrayed. We are taught that we should be able to sit absolutely still in absolute mind-blankness for hours on end. Then, and only then, have we succeeded.

Nonsense!

First of all, there is no "succeeding" in meditation. If we are entering into meditation to "do it right", we are already beginning on a false platform. And, if we are feeling unsuccessful at it, or like we're not capable of meditating, then we're hurting our own progress and lowering our vibration.

That is why it's important to begin from a positive perspective.

Why do we want to quiet our minds?

With meditation, we *do* want to quiet the mind. We want to rid ourselves of what I call "mind clutter", those thoughts that circle and circle our heads and reach every possible void of quietness we might seek. Any time we meditate and free ourselves from mind clutter for even just one second, we have gained from the experience.

Any decrease in mind clutter is an increase in our vibration.

On a practical, earthly level, we want to quiet our minds because it is those extra words spinning around that distract us, pull our energy down, allow us to worry and brood, encourage us to imagine potential negative situations and obsess over relationship details, and cause us to self-doubt ... What if all

---

If we feel unsuccessful at meditation, or like we're not capable of it, then we're hurting our own progress and lowering our vibration.

> Any time we meditate and free ourselves from mind clutter for even just one second, we have gained from the experience.

its presence but also stating it is not needed at this time, or c.) intending to stay in your higher self and simply allowing the ego to fall away.

2. Create white light in your mind.

Imagine white light coming down from heaven and surrounding you. Continually picture it brighter and whiter. Feel it coursing through your body. Take time to savor the feelings and absorb it as real. Allow the lightness of this vibration to fill your being.

When you feel fully saturated with this white light, focus on projecting it outward from your heart. Allow yourself to share with the universe what is all of ours. This giving will continue to increase and increase your vibration.

I find this technique works particularly well for me because I am able to focus on something, rather than attempt to not focus. I also find that I am able to re-tap into the blissful feeling this brings easier and more quickly the more I practice it.

3. Thoughts as feathers.

As you begin to quiet the thoughts in your mind, imagine that each thought is a feather. As it comes into your consciousness, picture it floating in and then gently blow it away. Each time a thought comes in, repeat the gentle action. Keep your actions and your thoughts soft, and allow rather than force.

In summary, find whatever method works best for you to turn down the noise — and turn up your frequency!

that energy was put to a better use?

On a spiritual plane, we want to quiet our minds because it is in those moments of quiet when we are able to better receive guidance and answers to our questions and to feel supported and loved by God and the universe.

Worrying versus feeling loved and supported = lowering our vibration versus raising our vibration.

Handling the Voices

There are many techniques for training ourselves to minimize mind clutter. We are all different — try these, or create your own process until you find the right fit.

1. Acknowledge that mind clutter is part of the "ego", and then put it aside.

This can mean a.) putting it in a box and "depositing" it aside from your mind's eye, b.) thanking it for

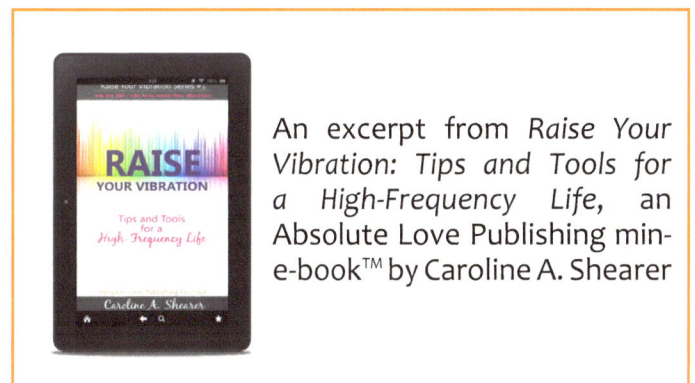

An excerpt from *Raise Your Vibration: Tips and Tools for a High-Frequency Life*, an Absolute Love Publishing mini-e-book™ by Caroline A. Shearer

CLEARING ENERGY
with Your Divine Self

An excerpt from *Personal Power through Awareness*
written by Sanaya Roman, channeling Orin

Sanaya Roman has been channeling Orin, a wise and gentle spirit teacher, for many years. One of Sanaya and Orin's greatest gifts is empowering intuitive and energetically open people to appreciate their sensitivity as a gift (and not a problem or a handicap) and that this gift is in fact, a powerful and reliable way to receive direct and divine information to make life-changing choices. In the newly revised bestselling spiritual classic **Personal Power Through Awareness: A Guidebook for Sensitive People** — the second book in the tremendously popular *Earth Life Series* — there are easy-to-follow processes that thousands have learned to create immediate and profound changes in their lives and relationships.

We hope you'll enjoy this excerpt from the newly revised section of the book.

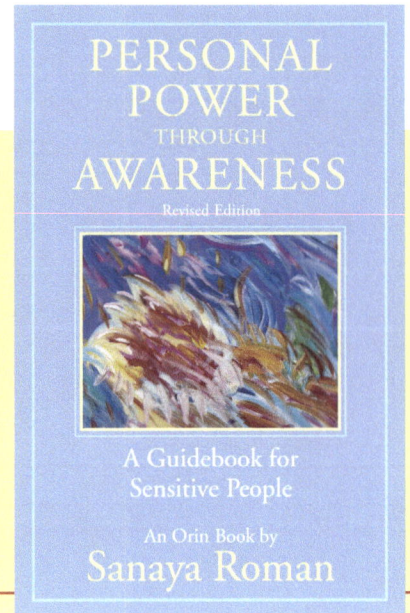

PERSONAL POWER THROUGH AWARENESS
Revised Edition
A Guidebook for Sensitive People
An Orin Book by
Sanaya Roman

Releasing and clearing energy is not just a mental exercise. It happens through increasing your inner light and working with your true, innermost divine Self. To get results, you will need to make a real connection to your divine Self and not just read about doing so. Use the playsheet that follows to learn how to connect with your divine Self and how to clear any energy you encounter.

What you consider to be a high, clear state today may be just a taste of how good you will feel as you continue connecting with your true, innermost Self and clear any energy that veils your inner light and truth. As your illumination increases, limiting thoughts and beliefs begin to dissolve, disappear, and no longer affect you, even if you are around them. When your energy is clear, you are magnetic to ideas, opportunities, inspiration, abundance, and people. Disharmony turns into harmony, turmoil into peace, self-doubt into self-confidence, and self-pity into self-esteem.

Playsheet:
Clearing Energy with Your Divine Self

This is a summary of the steps involved in clearing energy. Use this as a guide for the exercises on clearing that follow. The process of clearing does not need to take long. Once you learn these steps, you can apply them in a few short moments. The most important step is to make contact with your divine Self to increase your inner light.

1 **Set your intention** to recognize and clear any energy that is keeping you from experiencing the radiance, joy, love, and harmony that is your true nature.

2 **Think of something to clear.** Let a thought, memory, belief, or feeling come to mind that you would like to clear, something that is causing you stress or an out-of-balance feeling.

3 **Connect with your divine Self.** In a moment of inner peace and stillness, connect with your divine Self. You can do this in a few seconds, although taking longer is good as well. You might say, "I am open, I am receptive, I am asking for help to clear (whatever you want)." Pause for a moment in stillness and wait. Even 10 to 20 seconds is all you need to make contact and receive a response. Note that contact happens in a moment beyond words and thoughts, so you may have no awareness of making contact or receiving a response. Your intention to connect with your divine Self and your receptivity to It are all that is needed to make this connection and receive energy back. Know that your divine Self is aware of your desire to connect and always responds.

4 **Sense your inner light.** Imagine this connection to your divine Self filling you with light. You might picture this light as a pillar, column, or channel of light that runs through the middle of your body, around your spine. It rises straight up to your divine Self. This inner light shines out from you like a light bulb shines out. Your inner light shines brightly.

5 **Realize these energies can have no power over you.** As you shine your inner light upon whatever you want to clear, recognize that this energy has no power because it is not supported by any spiritual law or truth. You do not need to fight it or work hard to push it away.

6 **Impersonalize these energies; do not identify with them.** Affirm that these unwanted thoughts and feelings are not you. They are energies you have picked up from mass consciousness. In order to release these, it is important not to identify with them but to simply view them as impersonal energies that exist "out there."

7 **Turn them into nothing.** The light of your divine Self shining through you reveals the nothingness of all lesser, lower energies. There is no need to get rid of them, because they never existed. They are like the mirage in the desert that only seems real until you approach it. They are inconsequential, temporary, transitory energies that are easy to dissipate. Watch them fade into nothingness in the light you are holding upon them.

Evaluation

Notice whether anything has shifted, even in a small or subtle way, in how you feel or think about that area or situation. Perhaps you feel less worried or concerned, or it feels like some burden has been lifted. You may have a better feeling or feel physically more relaxed as you think of it. You may not be as drawn to think about that particular issue anymore, and other issues now seem more important. And you may forget about your concerns altogether.

Because you live in a world of time, the story you have about an area — your thoughts and feelings about it — will often shift over time, and you may not immediately experience the full results of your clearing work. However, the clearing you have done is real, and the work is cumulative. Every time you clear energy, you reduce the number of things you need to clear in the future.

You do not have to spend a lot of time clearing; in fact, it is very effective to have frequent 10- or 20-second periods of divine Self contact throughout the day, or whenever you notice you have taken on energy that you want to release. Do this even if it is a single thought or worry; take the time to clear it so it does not attract more of the same.

Learning to Love Myself

LORELEI SHELLIST

Some people see life as an adventure, while others see it as a scary ride. I've learned it can be both, but it doesn't have to be. The spirit of our journey is our choice to make, and it all centers on how uplifted we are by self-love.

Self-love doesn't come easily to all of us, especially later in life. Traumas and heartbreak sometimes turn us away from ourselves, or life's events cause us to learn to place other people's needs in front of our own. We can get better at loving ourselves, however, by turning our attention toward us through a practice of dedicated self-care.

I left home at a very young age to pursue my dreams of modeling. That taught me how to take care of life, but learning to take care of me was entirely different. In truth, it was a stumbling path at first as I had put so many things ahead of my peace and happiness. But today, I am much better at coping with whatever trials come my way, because I utilize a daily self-care practice that keeps me sure-footed along my journey.

I learned this approach while earning a masters' degree in spiritual psychology, and it has been such a blessing to me along my winding life path. While I engage in most of the below activities throughout the day, mornings are especially important to my self-care practice. To ensure I give myself the support and love I need, I get up early so I can treasure this sacred time uninterrupted. You can pick whatever moments feel most authentic to you.

A Daily Practice for Self-Care

Awaken with Gratitude

Wake up and before opening your eyes say a prayer of gratitude. Rise from bed, and move into your normal routine (whether that's by starting a pot of coffee, brewing a cup of tea, or jumping into the shower). Afterward, light a candle and say another prayer of thanks to anchor the feeling of gratitude into your day.

State Your Intentions

Listen to your inner voice and hear its wisdom. Recite your affirmations, and state your intentions for the day with a focus on cementing your inner voice's light. Take a moment to visualize your dreams as if you were already living them.

Free Your Mind

Take out a blank sheet of paper and spend at least 10 minutes writing down whatever is weighing on your mind. Write with abandon. Don't read what you're writing, and don't share it with anyone else. Just let the words flow from your mind out through your pen and onto the paper. Allow any negative thoughts, fears, or feelings to flow out with them.

Center Your Soul

Throughout the day, make it a point to center your soul. Read something uplifting and educational and let the message permeate your being. Pray and

> Traumas and heartbreak sometimes turn us away from ourselves, or life's events cause us to learn to place other people's needs in front of our own.

thank your higher being for the good things that have come your way, a goal you've reached, or the people you love. Schedule time for meditation, either at home or at work or while walking. Forgive yourself for any negative thoughts or for making irrational judgments of yourself or others. Send blessings to all your loved ones and let your love permeate out into the world.

Nurture Your Body

Make time to do the things that bring your body joy. Go for a swim, enjoy a yoga class, or take a walk around the block and notice the flowers, the birds, and the trees. Take quality vitamins, drink organic protein shakes, and eat non-processed, healthy foods. Take naps as often as your body needs.

Boost Your Confidence

Internal confidence often (at least initially and temporarily) stems from external confidence. To boost external confidence, take pride in your appearance and dress to impress. (My versatile dress, The Dream Dress®, was specifically designed to help women solve the eternal challenge of "what to wear" while flattering all shapes and sizes.) Then, to build and enhance your internal confidence, do at least one thing each day that you do well and enjoy doing. Also, make sure to congratulate yourself on progress made toward important goals. Write down at least two or three "wins" at the end of each day that made you feel especially good.

Share Your Vision

Write a blog or an email or a text to connect with and inspire others. Create or implement something meaningful to you and the world. Make connecting with clients or colleagues and sharing your services and talents a priority.

Honor Your Heart

Schedule dedicated time to connect with loved ones. Check in with your spouse, kids, parents, or friends and just listen to them. Give them your full, undivided attention. Tell them how proud you are of them and how blessed you feel to share life with them. Make self-honoring choices and agreements

Forgive yourself for any negative thoughts or for making irrational judgments of yourself or others. Send blessings to all your loved ones and let your love permeate out into the world.

with them while speaking from your heart.

Partaking in these daily practices can help you feel nurtured and cared for on a consistent basis. If you find you're struggling to stay committed to a daily practice of self-care, try tracking your activities for a month or more. I keep a monthly calendar called a Self-Nurturing Tracking Sheet. At the top, I write my name, the start date, and my goal or focus for the month (such as joy, abundance, peace, or courage). On the next line I write an affirmation related to that goal or focus, and below that I create a list of the activities (like the ones above) that I plan to do each day to nurture and love myself. I then make a checkmark next to each of the practices on the days I do them. At the end of the month, I get a visual log of my progress.

Your tracking sheet can look however you'd like, but the goal is to ensure it will show you where you are out of balance and remind you of what you need to be doing to support yourself. Remember: You may not get to do everything on your list every day and that's okay. Doing even at least some of these things on a regular, consistent basis will put you on the road to self-love. And, that is the road that leads you joyfully to wherever you want to go.

Lorelei Shellist is the author of *Runway Runaway: A Backstage Pass to Fashion, Romance and Rock 'n Roll* and designer of The Dream Dress®. She also is a contributor to *Love Like God* and *Women Will Save the World*. Buy the dress collection at runwayrunawaycollection.com.

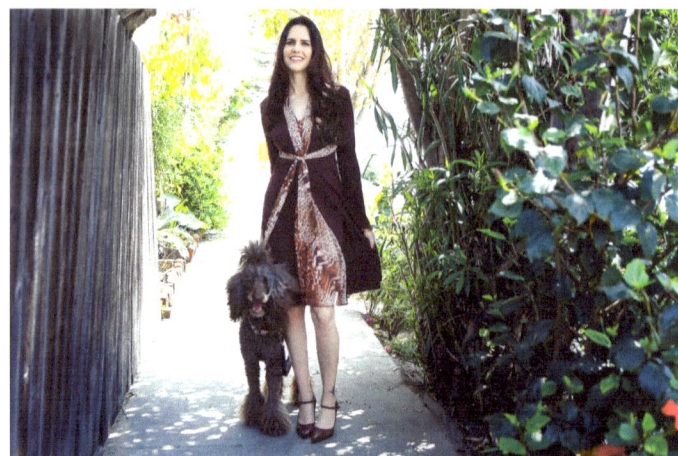

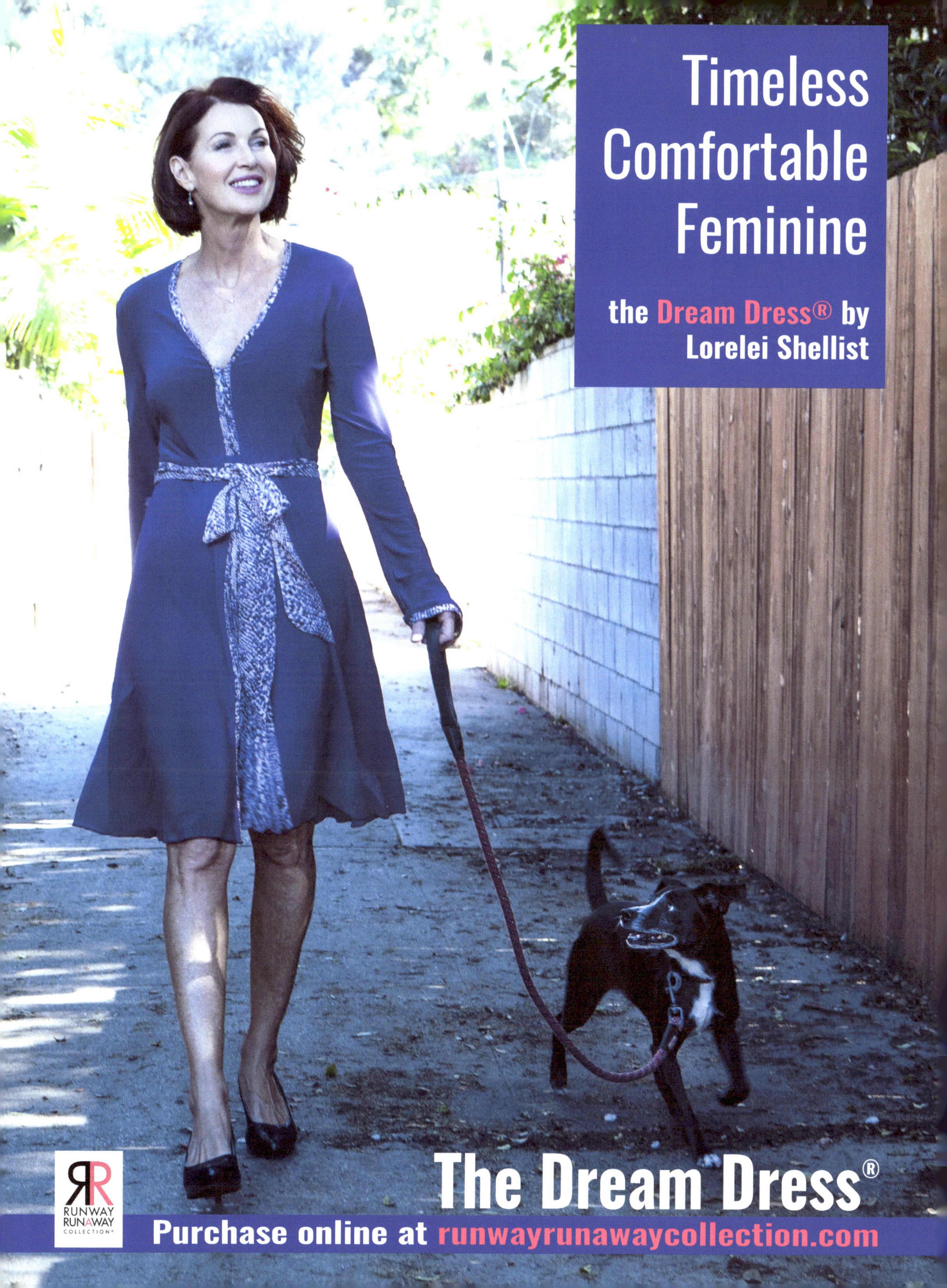
Timeless
Comfortable
Feminine
the Dream Dress® by
Lorelei Shellist
RUNWAY
RUNAWAY
COLLECTION
The Dream Dress®
Purchase online at runwayrunawaycollection.com

Romantic Relationships
from a Spiritual Perspective

Romantic relationships offer us the potential to evolve our souls in dramatic and intimate ways. Sometimes these relationships are brief and powerful. Sometimes they are long and quiet but leave an indelible mark on our souls.

When two people come together in lifelong partnership, it is a blessing enabling them to learn and ultimately embody unconditional love. The couple is gifted with a lifetime to honor each other as separate beings and to unite as one.

Each day two people remain in love is a day that love blossoms, not only for themselves but for everyone. For as one loves more, the world loves more. And this is the beauty of love, that it is infinite in abundance.

When we are blessed with romantic relationships of any length or strength, we can choose to recognize what purpose these relationships may be serving our souls. Once we are able to see a larger purpose, it helps us release some of the less loving emotions that may come up over the course of a relationship.

When we have caring feelings for others, we want the best for them. The challenge is wanting the best for them, while allowing the reality they choose to create – and allowing it gracefully, peacefully, and with full support.

When it may appear to us that others are making mistakes, we can appreciate that life is offering them growth lessons and applaud them for taking on these challenges. We can recognize that their souls are in a different – but equally valuable – place as ours and that these lessons are serving an equally valuable purpose.

When we feel others are causing us harm or pain, we can reevaluate our own boundaries and recognize that everyone's perception of reality is different. We can use moments of pain as moments to be grateful. When an area of sensitivity is brought out by someone else, we can thank them because we are now aware of an area within us that needs more love.

A large part of extending unconditional love to others is releasing attachment. This does not mean we release intimate relationships – we need those to grow. An evaluation of why we feel the need to have a certain response will bring the issue back to our own selves, where we can work through it with love.

When there are relationships that cause us discomfort because of a conditional love, it may be time to shift out of the relationship. Trust that when you are ready for a higher-love relationship, it will come to you. Also trust that you will remain in a conditional-love relationship as long as you are still learning what you are meant to learn.

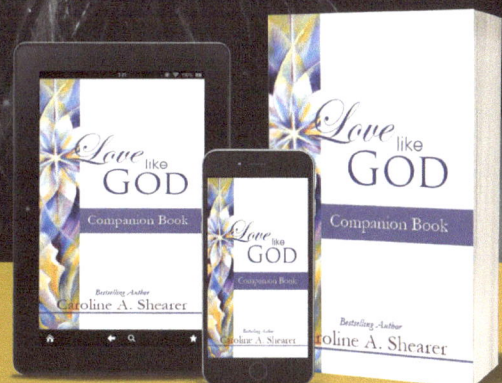

From *Love Like God Companion Book* by Caroline A. Shearer

let's

CONNECT
... for real

The Art of Being in the Moment

Eating watermelon with sticky hands in the sunshine. Relaxing on a porch while children play. Feeling soft grass beneath toes and feet.

Peaceful, grounded, earthy moments like these have been part of the human experience for all time. Whatever challenges the generations have felt, whatever ailments or fears, humans always have excelled at personal connection and being in the moment. Except, perhaps, for now.

If asked, could we honestly say the same is true today?

Technology has enhanced our lives for the better in an infinite number of ways, enabling us to connect with people and societies all across the globe in ways previous generations could never have imagined. Yet many people report feeling disconnected from themselves and others. Could it be that some of this technological connection is causing us to miss out on the connection that is ... well, real? In other words, are we so busy observing our moments that we have forgotten to step inside of them?

Wherever you are, whatever you are doing, be there, doing that.

Divas that Care Founder Candace Gish knows well the benefits that come from our technologically connected society. Her online network connects women around the world who are making positive changes in their communities. As wonderful as those connections are, however, Gish says it is important we not lose focus on what is right in front of us. "Some online connections are amazing and life-altering, but some — like the perpetual negativity found in a few online support groups or unleashed on various anonymous platforms — are bad for the spirit. And then some are just clutter that take us away from our best selves."

As an illustration, Gish said, social media is a wonderful tool to keep up with people we wouldn't be able to keep up with otherwise. It could be asserted, however, that while social media and other forms of technology don't diminish our human journey, they can diminish our interpretation of it. After all, our online perception of events is dramatically different than if we'd physically experienced those same events.

Compare the act of attending the funeral of a friend's parent, for example, to the act of clicking a sad face or writing an "I'm sorry" note on a social media website. Compare the emotions of watching a couple's first dance at their wedding to viewing an edited wedding album link with 300 photos online. Compare experiencing first-hand your child's hard-fought, tearful journey toward reaching a goal to simply posting a smiling "after" photo for others to "like" in support.

There are stark differences in the impact these things have on our emotional and intellectual selves. And while it, indeed, can be wonderful to have more information, we must put that information to good use. Otherwise, it's just a distraction that leads us further away from each other.

more from our human experience. We deserve to disconnect at least some of the time.

"When we are unencumbered by constant technological connection, we feel happier and less stressed. When we are living in the real, present moment, we can feel that we are living our best life without wanting for more. In that moment, we are not looking outside of ourselves for input or validation. We are not relying on what other people think of us. We're just existing, with each other, like we are meant to do."

She said stepping away from technology provides the space and freedom to get to know ourselves,

"Let's connect again for real," said Gish. "I think that is what I miss the most. I miss that face-to-face connection that occurs in the midst of real life, as a mom especially. Let's simply have dinner together with the TV off."

She said, "I am always running around with the kids, but I feel like we're never really connecting. As a society, we've created this constant need to rush, rush, rush and just do *more*. And we all fall prey to that, myself included. So even when we are spending time together, we often are not really present in the ways we could be. Quite frankly, we deserve

and each other, better. "Sometimes with social media, we don't feel like who we really are. We can be waiting for a notification, waiting for an update, or looking with rose-colored glasses at other people's lives. Let's not wait for that. Let's go live in the moment. Let's find out who we are through different kinds of experiences. Real-life experiences. Let's find out what makes us loveable, what makes us better people."

To connect and be more present in everyday life Gish offers these tips:

Use Social Media Genuinely.

• Spend less time on social media. Set a timer if you have trouble with this. For example, allow yourself 15 minutes to connect in the morning. Then, turn it off.

• Be aware of the tone of what you are viewing. Do you need to unfollow or hide certain people or pages? If you're consistently seeing negative ideas or actions, set a boundary to respect your mental and emotional health. Conversely, are there people or pages that light up your soul? Make a point to engage in those positive spaces rather than in the more negative realms.

• If you find yourself mindlessly scrolling and zoning out for hours on end, stop and walk away. As the saying goes, when it's all said and done you're never going to wish you'd had another chance to interact online.

• Review your motivations for looking at social media in the first place. Are you bored? Is your brain spinning? Rather than mask these emotions of unrest, do the work to address the core issue. Then, log on only when your desire is for real connection.

"Social media is not bad!" said Gish. "We just need to realize that our whole lives should not be in front of a computer. That's how we make better use of it."

Turn Off Your Notifications.

Gish believes it's important to harness our days so that we are in charge of them, not those constant dings and lights from our devices. This is why she's made it a point to turn off all of the notifications on her phone. "Can it not wait an hour?" she asked. "Almost always, it can. And if it can't, if it's a true emergency, someone will call."

• Set priority rings/notifications so that you can ensure you are available to those who truly need constant access to you

(such as your kids) while comfortably muting others.

• Consider taking social sites off your phone so that you have to make an effort to visit them.

• Have set "phone off" times for you and your family, such as during dinner and after a certain hour, so you can reconnect with each other in the real world on a regular basis.

Make Your People a Priority.

When we are constantly on our phones or computers or televisions, we are sending a message to our loved ones that they are not important enough to us. By putting our gadgets away, we show our people that they are needed and wanted in our lives. Otherwise, we rarely connect in a meaningful way over the course of the day.

"The relationships with our spouse, our children, our life partner — those are the relationships we've got to cultivate," said Gish. "Those are the people who need to feel wanted and needed by us, just like we do by them. Those are the people we should be nurturing and making consistent time for, not acquaintances we've met online."

Break Your Day into Segments.

Gish suggests planning out your day if you struggle with completing your daily tasks.

• Make checklists and stick to them.

• Break your day into seg-

ments, and include time for relaxation and no-guilt play!

• Be firm with your boundaries when intrusions come knocking.

• Exercise discipline with others to train them into understanding that your time and mental space are valuable.

"If I am not consciously aware of what I am doing at any given time, then I feel at the end of the day that I haven't accomplished anything," said Gish. "That leads to rushing around to finish things, which just leads to me feeling stressed and like I'm not present when I want to be."

Practice Centering Every Day.

"What do I want to achieve? What are my goals as a person? What traits do I want to embody? Those are the questions that can help us to re-center and re-focus on what is important to us," said Gish. "Doing that can go a long way toward helping us make better decisions the entire day. Often we are so overwhelmed with 'stuff' that we can't focus anymore."

• Practice affirmations daily.

• Focus on what is in front of you, in the moment.

• Have the discipline to stop and breathe consciously at least once a day, rather than continuing to go-go-go.

• Learn to recognize when your thoughts are going in circles and bring a cold halt to them.

Create Present Moments.

"It's important to understand that regardless of how connected we are technologically speaking, we still need basic human connection. We also need to realize that we can't do it all — at least not every day — and that is ok!"

Find what works for you and/or your family and friends to carve out moments where you all are truly present. Consider:

• Family dinner time

• Nightly walks

• Afternoon coffee or tea get-togethers

• Game nights

• Mother and son/father and daughter (and vice versa) "dates" for breakfast, etc.

• No-TV nights

Gish said that even though temporarily pulling away from technology can be difficult, the benefits are well worth it, not just for our own sake but for sake of the example we are setting for those around us as well. "If we say to our kids, 'Why are you not outside playing and riding your bikes?' while we stare at our phone, what example are we setting?" she asked. "Don't settle for that version of yourself. Experience what your best self can be. Get out there with them, and see if you can still ride a bike!"

Candace Gish is the founder of the Divas that Care movement, an engaged community of women creating positive change in the world and sharing their experiences as a way to support and uplift each other. Is your passion to create positive change in the world? Listen to the Divas that Care Podcast or apply to be a guest at www.divasthatcare.com.

Denise Thompson

CONNECT IN REAL LIFE:
Start an In-Person Share Group

In today's technologically driven world, it seems we're constantly plugged in, turned on, and connected to others in our neighborhoods and around the world. But are we? Ask almost anyone if they truly *feel* connected to others, and the answer is likely to be hazy at best.

Why is that? Perhaps it's as simple as this: Those polished pictures and self-edited posts just don't feel real.

We are social beings who need *genuine* connection — not just any connection. Pings, likes, and tweets aside, social media just doesn't feel authentic to most of us. We need more.

And that more isn't just about a greater number of connections. It's about *different* connections. We need balance in the types of connections we have in our lives.

Think about when anything is out of balance in life. What happens? You can't hold that new yoga pose, your checking account goes into overdraft, your personal life falls apart when work takes precedence, that second scoop of ice cream topples off the cone, and the server tray carrying your favorite meal crashes to the ground. Nothing good comes from imbalance.

Social media has its place. It enables us to keep up with relatives and friends and interest groups who are miles away. It gives the sick or those unable to leave their homes a path to connect with the outside world and those who truly understand what they're going through. Social media lets us share our proudest, most joyous, and most exciting moments with those we love. It also helps various social movements and health advocacy causes harness the power of an audience and build momentum for change. But those are just some types of the connections we humans need, and for too many of us those social media connections encompass the vast majority of all (if not all) of our daily connections with others.

In the simplest terms, our connectedness is out of balance. Thankfully, however, we can choose to usher balance back into our lives. We can put away the screens and take stock of the people around us. We can make an effort to have direct connection with people, in person, while keeping social media a smaller part of our social habits.

How do we do this?

One way is by starting an in-person Share Group. A Share Group is a fantastic way to start meeting the need for genuine connection that we all share. (And yes, before we get any further, it *does* have to be *in person*. That's the entire point!)

The Basics of Sharing

A Share Group is an informal, recurring, get-together that centers on a varying theme or idea. While each meeting's theme may differ, the point of each meeting remains the same: to connect. (This differs from a club, where the theme never changes and the topic is often more important than the opportunity for connection.) In a Share Group, the theme is simply a jumping-off point for discussion.

Topics can range from sharing useful or interest-ing life "hacks" to seeking advice to letting out difficult feelings. Regardless of what's discussed at any particular meeting, the overall idea is that everyone in attendance is heard and that the group feels like a judgment-free zone where all participants can relax, laugh, enjoy, cry, learn, reminisce, and offer and receive support. Hopefully, all while enjoying snacks and having a glass of sweet tea or wine!

In my own life, I've found Share Group meetings have helped me to voice unspoken fears, connect with others who are experiencing similar things, meet people who want to try the same hobby I do, and learn about great books, movies, and ideas. Most importantly, they have fostered direct, purposeful human contact that has helped me feel like I belong.

Interested in starting a Share Group of your own? It's easy!

The How-Tos

Step One: Pick your theme. Use your imagination here. There are no limits! Any unifying theme will work to kick off the chat. Once the conversation gets started, you will find it easily evolves into other topics, which naturally will offer ideas for the next meeting's theme.

Step Two: Invite friends, acquaintances, co-workers, or anyone you feel comfortable inviting. Think outside the box when planning! Inviting people of diverse ages, perspectives, etc. brings texture, rich-

With each new meeting, my emotional bank account receives a big deposit!

ness, and true authenticity to the group. And that's key to genuine connection.

Step Three: Organize and distribute information. Here's where technology actually can help foster authentic connection! Use that social media for good. Invite people to a private page on your favorite platform where you can pick meeting dates and times, vote on future topics, and welcome new members to your tribe. (Yep, I said it — you now have a tribe!) Use this online gathering spot to grow your group or keep it small. Whatever works for you and your group.

Step Four: Keep it positive. Keep your discussions real, but stay focused on maintaining a positive group vibe. A Share Group is meant to be a positive force in life. Yes, you can vent or share a worry and lean on a true friend made, but keep in mind Share Groups are not meant for gossip, complaining, judgment, or other lower vibrational habits.

Step Five: Connect, and have fun! That's it! Honest.

Still worried about finding a theme? Don't be! Anything will do, especially the first time around. But just in case you're really stuck, here are a few possible themes to get you started:

Favorite Product Show-and-Tell: Everyone brings a favorite product to share with the group.

The Swap: Everyone brings a box of gently used items to swap with the group, sort of like a free garage sale. (This has been one of the most popular Share Groups themes in my group!) To keep things simple and balanced, you can limit ahead of time the number of items each person can bring. Ten is often a good number. Or you can say there is no limit on certain items, like books or puzzles, and specify that any items not claimed will go to a senior care center or other local organization after the event.

Favorite Podcast: Everyone downloads or bookmarks a favorite podcast or two, and then shares a snippet via phone or another device.

Hobby Night: Everyone brings photos or items centered on a favorite hobby or a new hobby they'd like to try. This easily can connect like-minded people with similar passions and even start life-long friendships.

Pet Love: Everyone brings pet photos and a pet story to share. The conversations will be endless!

Most Embarrassing Moment: You know that thing you did that you never, ever talk about? In a trusted group, you can be brave and share that moment you thought you'd never share. You will laugh (and maybe shed a tear or two!) but it will feel good to finally release it. Just be prepared with a few icebreakers to get more reserved members in the mood to share.

Group Field Trip: Meet at a place/restaurant/cafe you've always wanted to visit but have never had the chance to try in order to experience a change from the normal routine and make new memories.

Open Mic Night: Any topic is up for conversation at this meeting!

Still worried about running out of ideas? Ask for help! At each meeting, leave out some paper, a few pens, and an idea bowl for group members to drop in their own ideas for the next event's theme.

There really are no limits to what can be a "theme" for a Share Group. I honestly can say that I have truly loved every gathering I've attended, regardless of what we talked about each time. That's because, at each event, I always meet new people, get new ideas, reminisce fondly, and belly laugh like you would not believe! To me, that's the point.

Investing time in people-to-people contact has been hugely rewarding. With each new meeting, my emotional bank account receives a big deposit! And it's wonderful to consistently have something enjoyable and real to look forward to attending.

Your turn! Decide how to invite your soon-to-be tribe, pick a starter theme, play the host(ess), and watch those connections evolve. You'll be so glad you gave it a try. Trust me!

18 Incredible Journeys by Young Female Changemakers
Committed to Making a Difference in Our World

YOUNG
Divas
THAT CARE

COMPILED BY
CANDACE GISH

A *Divas* THAT CARE BOOK

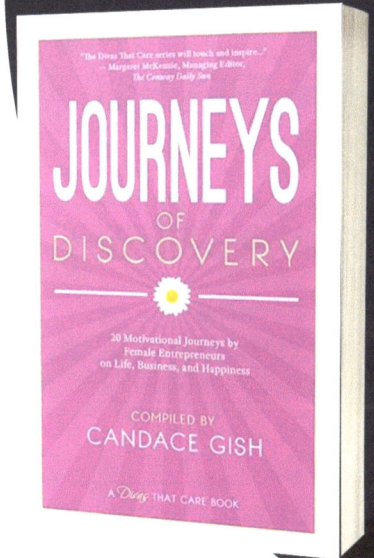

Animal Speak

How Harnessing Animal Messages Can Improve Our Lives

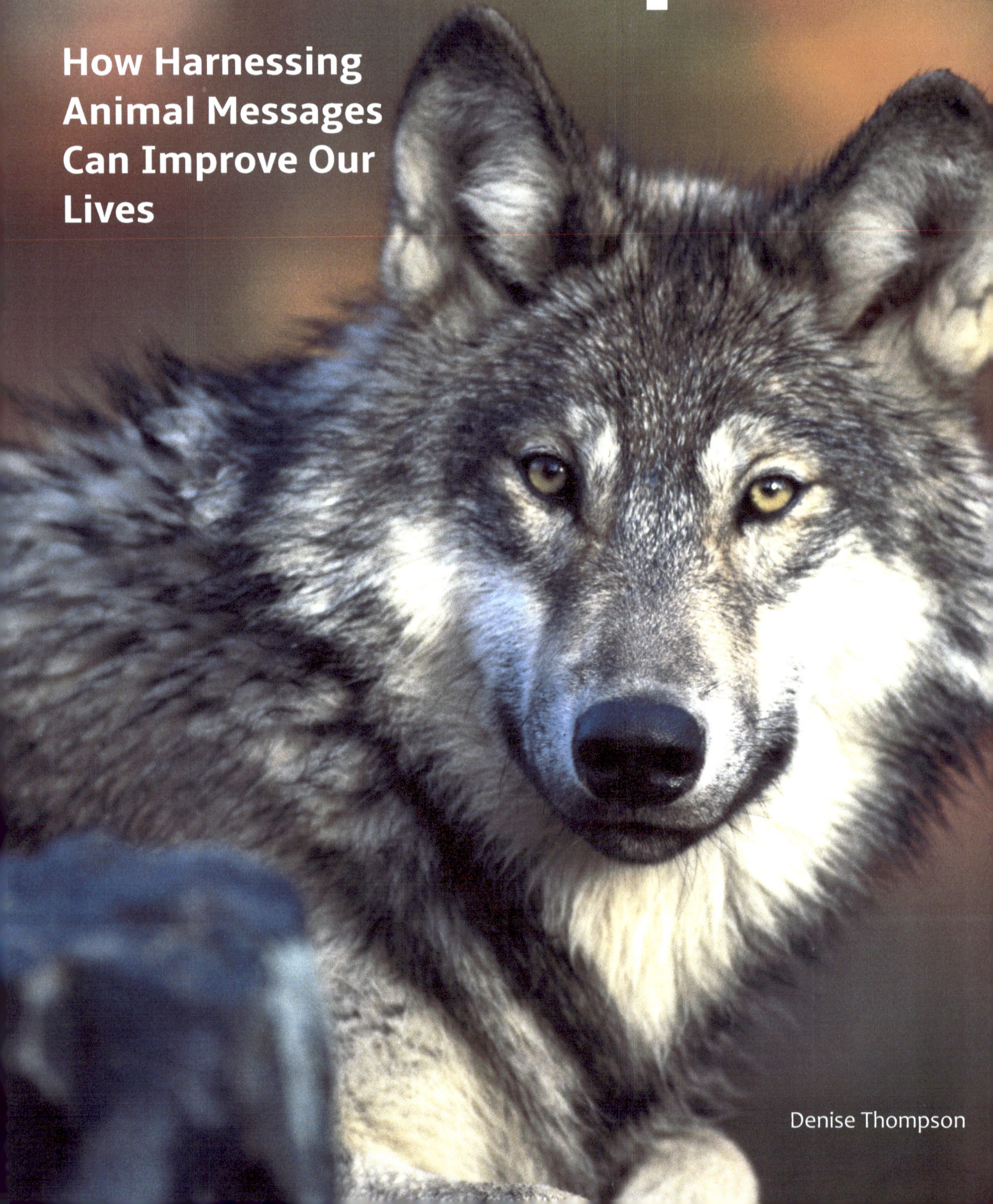

Denise Thompson

Animals are an important part of many of our lives. They may be our companions for the unconditional love we crave to give and receive or they may provide their loyalty and intelligence as service animals. According to Ted Andrews' *Animal Speak*, however, animals may also be messengers bringing gifts of healing, protection, power, and inspiration to humanity.

"As humans, we sometimes forget that we can starve as much from a lack of wonder as we can a lack of food. When we open ourselves to animals and Nature, we open our hearts and souls to true wonders," wrote Andrews.

Animals may bring their intended messages to us in our dreams or meditations or by showing up in our lives and in nature. When animals appear repeatedly, we can feel sure there is a message intended for us. Figuring out what that message is can be tricky, however.

The first thing we can do is to focus on the moment the animal appeared to us and ask ourselves a few essential questions: "What was I doing? What was going on in my life for which I needed guidance? What *might* the message have been?"

Just taking the time to notice the animal's appearance, acknowledge its appearance, and think about the possibility of a message opens our minds to allow thoughts and answers to come forward. Journaling or keeping notes on such events also can be helpful, as we sometimes see things more clearly or are more likely to recognize patterns in hindsight.

According to *Animal Speak*, there are five categories of animal messengers: Healers, Protectors, Personal Power Animals, Message Bringers, and Teachers.

Healers

Healers are animals that can provide healing for yourself and others. For example, the butterfly is known for transformation and new beginnings. If you are going through relationship, occupation, or other big life changes, you may find a message in learning about the strengths and characteristics of butterflies.

Protectors

These animals alert us to be strong and to analyze a situation or person in our lives. Look at the characteristics of this animal, and keep in mind that they don't necessarily have to be big animals — each creature has a way to protect itself no matter the size. Andrews provides the example of an opossum, from which the term "playing possum" is derived. Maybe someone or something is not who or how you think they are, and it is time to think more pro-

> As humans, we sometimes forget that we can starve as much from a lack of wonder as we can a lack of food.

tectively of yourself. If this feels like it is the case, take some time to observe the person or situation before making decisions.

Personal Power Animals

Have you noticed an animal or animals showing up on a recurring basis in your life or your dreams? Has it been your whole life, or maybe just as you go through difficult situations? Make special note of these animals. Analyze their characteristics and symbolism to see where they might apply to you or your situation. Also, consider that they may be introducing a trait that would be helpful for you to adopt.

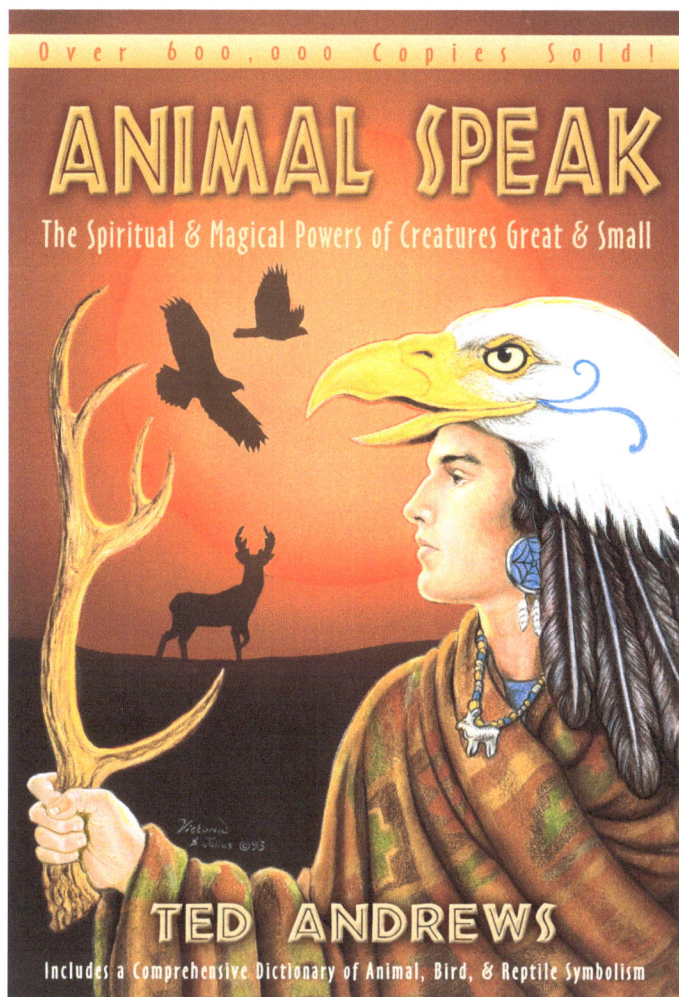

> No matter how much we cloak ourselves in civilization, we will always be a part of Nature.
> ~ Ted Andrews

Message Bringers

These animals appear to us in order to guide and give us direction in our lives. For example, if a robin appears, think about the renewal and growth a new season brings — and how you can apply those principles to this phase of your life. Maybe try something new!

Teachers

When teachers appear, there is something we are meant to learn. In this case, ask, "What am I being shown?" Perhaps the message is to remind us about a characteristic we are not calling upon within ourselves. For example, cows are a symbol of nourishment, fertility, and new birth. If we see cows, we may need to learn that we must nourish and take care of ourselves first before we can be at our best to care for others.

Now that you know the main categories of animals that can herald messages, let's look at some common animals and what they may mean. You may never have considered that these animals — which include birds, insects, aquatic life, amphibians and lizards, and arachnids — may be offering you a message!

Keep in mind that many animals have more than one meaning, share meanings with other animals, and fall into more than one category. It is also worth noting that different cultures and/or belief systems may have varied meanings and characteristics for each animal.

Animals and Their Meanings

BLUE JAY (CHOOSE WISELY)
Be careful of the choices you make. Choose so others do not get hurt. Don't be afraid. Stay with the choices you have made.

BLACKBIRD (PROTECT WHAT'S YOURS)
Usually a good sign of promise, it is important to stake out your territory. The forces of Nature are with you now.

CARDINAL (RENEWED IMPORTANCE)

Accept your life's importance. Accept yourself as a source of light, and do not be afraid to conduct yourself accordingly.

SWAN (MAGICAL WONDERS)

Magical realms are opening. Trust in your heart, your true self, and your creativity. New opportunities are coming.

BUTTERFLY (NEW BIRTH)

New love and joy are coming. Transformation is inevitable but will be easier than expected. Embrace new beginnings.

BROWN SPIDER (SLOW HEALING)

Examine close, personal relationships. Deal with hidden hurts and betrayals from the past. Time will help heal.

COCKROACH (ADAPTABILITY)

Be adaptable and sensitive to subtle changes. Adaptability is essential in all environments now. Be flexible, and adapt to outside pressures.

MOSQUITO (SELF-WORTH)

Protect yourself against attacks on your self-worth. Irritations and unresolved issues become aggravating. Focus on personal joys.

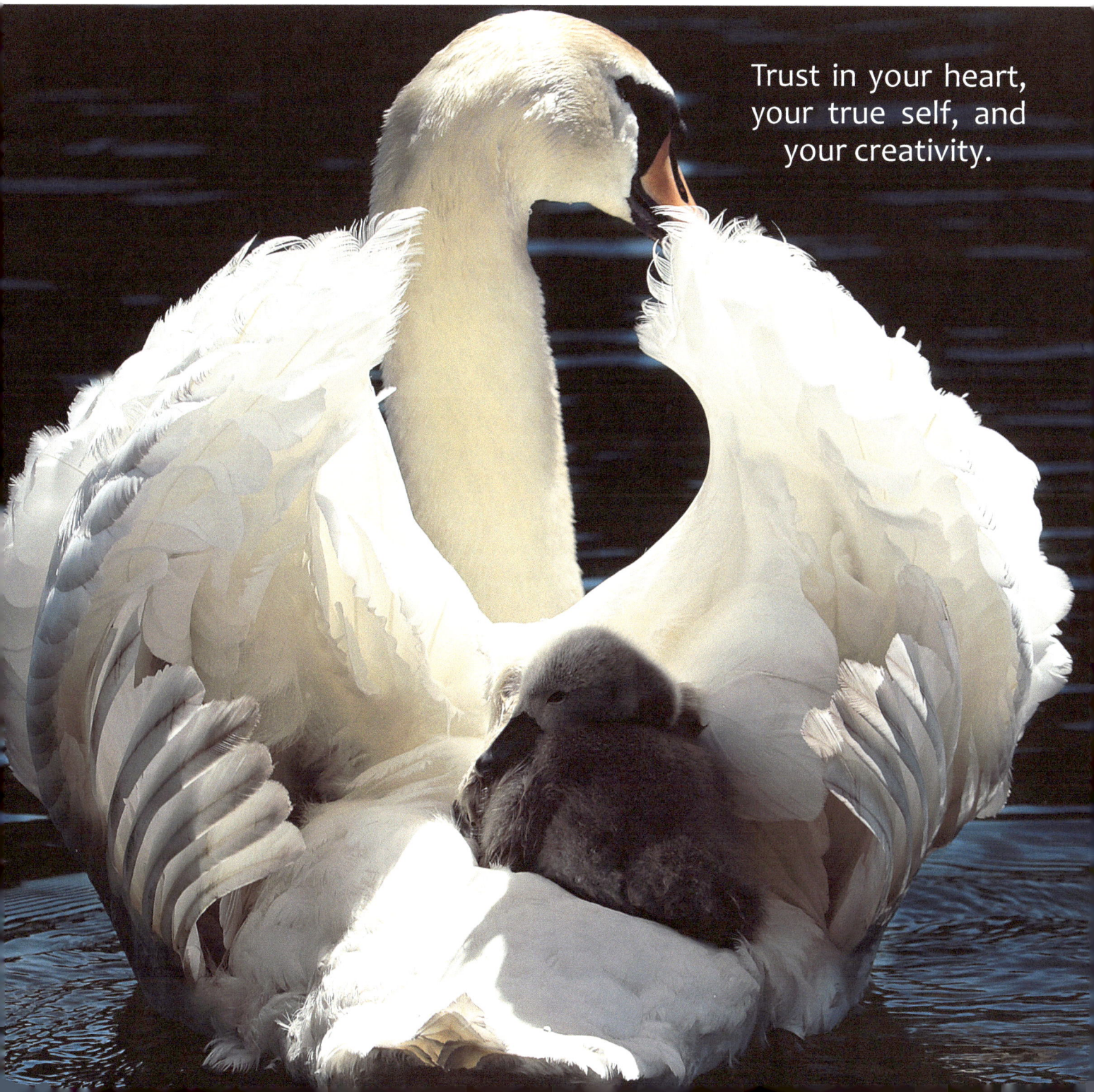

Trust in your heart, your true self, and your creativity.

DRAGONFLY (TIME TO SHINE)

Trust in the power of your light and your perception to succeed. Efforts are maturing. A spiritual path is ahead.

DEER (LURE TO ADVENTURES)

Move gently into new areas. Follow the lure to new studies. Practical pursuits bring surprising rewards.

DOG (FAITHFULNESS)

Be faithful and alert to protect endeavors and those closest to you. Look at your companionship as it relates to your success.

MOUSE (DETAILS)

Focus on the details. Attend to the little things that will lead to bigger opportunities. Do not allow your attention to be distracted.

WOLF (GUIDANCE)

Though not apparent yet, change is occurring. Trust in yourself to find your path. Take control. Protection surrounds you in journeys.

CAT (INDEPENDENCE)

Mystery and magic are afoot, but you must find your own way of expressing them. Develop your ability to be more independent.

GARTER SNAKE (ACT)

Act on as many ideas as possible, but do not become overstressed. This is not the time to sit on ideas. Inspiration flows.

LIZARD (SUBTLE PERCEPTIONS)

Pay attention to dreams and psychic perceptions. Do not be afraid to detach from problems. Sepa-

Move gently into new areas. Practical pursuits bring surprising rewards.

rate, and do what you must.

TORTOISE (MOVE THROUGH PRESSURE)

Pressures are easing and movement is slow but steady. Things will happen in the time and manner best for you. Focus on essentials.

SEA SHELL (FEMININE POWER)

There is sound coming forth of new life, like the trumpeting in a conch shell. Prepare for a journey to a new and protected life.

CARP (BLESSED LOVE)

Opportunities for achievement are on the horizon, especially in love and relationships. Do not ignore what is essential.

STARFISH (FOLLOW YOUR OWN PATH)

Follow your own unique path. Do what is right for you, no matter how difficult. It will bring stars of rewards and possibilities.

As children, we never missed seeing or pointing out animals or the ways in which nature grabbed our attention (ways we often overlook as adults). Keep in touch with messages from nature and with your inner child to allow the intrigue, healing, and energizing guidance of animal messages to be present in your life. And when you feel unsure about making a decision, ask for guidance. See which critters appear after your request, and heed their messages!

The animal message definitions and concepts above are based on Ted Andrews' *Animal Speak* and *Animal-Speak Pocket Guide*, which includes hundreds more animal messages from exotic animals, birds, insects, aquatic life, amphibians and lizards, arachnids, and more. Reprinted with permission.

Trust in the power of your light and your perception to succeed.

Denise Thompson is the Ambassador at Absolute Love Publishing, where she supports the promotion of all of our endeavors, helping to inspire joy in our team and in our myriad readers, clients, and authors, as well as sharing our message with the world.

CHARGE UP and REJUVENATE
with Earthing

Kicking off our shoes at the end of a long day not only feels good, it can be good *for* us. In addition to spreading out the toes, removing our shoes stimulates more than 7,000 nerve endings on the bottom of each foot. Our brains interpret the signals from these nerve endings to help us have better balance and coordination. Better yet, when we walk barefoot on the ground, we naturally reconnect, relax, and recharge our bodies in an ancient practice known as *earthing*.

What Is Earthing?

Earthing is a technique of grounding one's body to the earth via bare-skin contact, and it is highly effective at calming, energizing, and restoring us to our naturally present state. Examples of earthing

have effectively caused us to become ungrounded. When we aren't grounded, our stressed energies have no outlet and so they tend to get stored as inflammation. Earthing reconnects us to the earth, enabling us to plug ourselves into its energy source and recharge in the same way plugging our cell phones into a charger fills the phone's battery. And because the earth has a greater negative charge than our bodies carry, we wind up absorbing the electrons that are continually being given off by its surface. After only 20 to 30 minutes of "recharging", inflammation is released and energy is renewed.

Get the Best Effects Near Water

There's a reason why 100 percent of people feel better by the ocean: Everyone at the beach is barefoot and walking on damp sand (the best natural conductor of the earth's electrons), while also enjoying calming negative ions coming in off the ocean breeze. It's a perfect prescription for relaxing and rejuvenating one's physical body.

It is believed that when we absorb these negatively charged electrons, their electrical charge helps improve the structure of the water in our cells. Basically, structured water is how water exists in nature, when it comes bubbling to the earth's surface from a natural spring — before it has been mechanically processed in any way. In this natural state, its molecules are lined up in a neat and orderly fashion.

Structured-water enthusiasts claim this unadulterated water is vibrantly alive and holds more energy than loosely or non-structured water as it's created from the light, heat, and movement water naturally experiences outdoors. Examples of these vortex-inducing energies include sunlight, underground pressure, and the agitation that occurs as water flows and whirls along in a stream or waterfall. These energies electrically infuse the water with a negative charge as they structure its molecular shape, which makes it easier for this type of water to enter and hydrate our cells.

Scientists have studied places famous for their healing waters, such as Lourdes in France, Ecuador's mountain streams, and the high glacial rivers found in the Himalayan Mountains. All of these regions have long been known as places where people experience unusual longevity and vitality. What's more, all of these magical waters have been found to be alkaline and to carry a negative electrical charge.

In his book, *The Fourth Phase of Water*, biomedical engineer Dr. Gerald Pollack, a recognized pio-

JEAN BRANNON

are walking barefoot outside; gardening without gloves; sitting or lying outside on a sheet; and even taking a lawn chair out into the yard, slipping off our shoes, and placing our feet on the grass.

The advent of modern shoes (with their energy-blocking soles) and modern homes (often built on energy-disconnecting crawl spaces or over basements and floors covered in sealers or carpeting)

Getting stressed tends to make us shallow breathers and compulsive worriers. As a result, our energies rise to the head, leaving us feeling foggy and ungrounded.

neer in the science behind structured water, reveals that these healing structured waters have a similar "honeycomb" shape to those found in healthy cells. This shape creates a barrier preventing pollutants, toxins, and unwanted particles from penetrating the cell wall. Conversely, Pollack also found that diseased cells had a much weaker negative charge, and when dying, lost their structure quickly — which meant they lost their natural resistance to keeping out toxins.

Just as these tests have shown that water will structure itself when a negative charge is introduced, earthing appears to work primarily by pulling our cellular water back into its healthy, naturally structured form. And so when we practice earthing on a regular basis, our tissues are supplied with a healing hydration that yields these three major, feel-good benefits:

Feel-Good Benefit #1: Earthing Reconnects Scattered Energies

When life feels busy or stressful, we tend to over-think, overplan, and overwork. From a Chinese medicine perspective, this type of overdoing can tax the lung and spleen meridians. Since the lung provides the body's strongest descending force and the spleen feeds worry when it's out of balance, getting stressed tends to make us shallow breathers and compulsive worriers. As a result, our energies rise to the head, leaving us feeling foggy and ungrounded. By earthing 20 to 30 minutes daily or at least a few times a week, we can ground the lung and settle the spleen, leading to enhanced vibrancy. (This is especially true if we also add in some deep belly breathing.)

Feel-Good Benefit #2: Earthing Drains and Relaxes Nervous Tension

Chronic stress is rampant in the United States. According to a 2017 Gallup poll, eight in 10 Americans reported feeling too much pressure in their daily lives. In Chinese medicine, we usually see excess tension showing up as tight neck and shoulder muscles, irritability, and headaches, which are all signs of an out-of-balance liver meridian. Once earthing grounds the lungs (which helps to release any built-up inflammation our bodies have stored), our breath can then power the liver to move energy more freely and easily throughout the body. It's this ease of energy movement that allows the liver to be soothed, resulting in less stress and strain.

Feel-Good Benefit #3: Earthing Recharges Our Inner Batteries

Over the long haul, stress can deplete our backup reserves, effectively draining our tanks and leading to feelings of exhaustion and chronic fatigue. Chinese medicine associates our deepest restorative energies with the kidney meridian. By practicing earthing 20 to 30 minutes daily or at least a few times a week, the electrons so freely emanating from the earth allow a tired kidney channel to undergo much-needed restoration.

Best Way to Add Earthing to Daily Life

Even though there are many ways to approach earthing — including devices such as mats, sheets, and shoes that can help us get grounded — there's no more effective way for folks to experience the benefits earthing offers than by doing it the old-fashioned way: bare feet to the ground or bare hands in the garden. These methods are unbeatable for their ability to help us reconnect, relax, and recharge — all in just 20 to 30 minutes per day.

Earthing and Grounding Meditation

Time to practice! Pick a peaceful spot outdoors. If the weather is cold and rainy, or if it's snowing, you may wish to try bundling up on a covered patio with an unfinished concrete surface (bare concrete won't block the electron absorption process). A garage or basement might be other sheltered options. If the weather is pretty outside, I recommend taking a lawn chair out into the grass or spreading a sheet on the ground. Of course, sitting with your back against a tree is a fine way to ground yourself, too!

Once you are lying down or seated comfortably, focus on taking deep, centering belly breaths. Inhale and exhale slowly and rhythmically, imagining purple and gold tree roots extending down from your feet and anchoring into the very core of the earth.

Draw purple and gold energy up from the earth, so it ascends your legs and hugs your heart in a secure embrace. From the heart, let these energies reach out along your arms and into your fingertips, which you also can imagine growing purple and gold roots that extend down and anchor into the earth.

Once you feel grounded, envision the purple and gold roots rising up from your heart, out through the top of your head, and then wrapping around the sun — drawing its golden light down into and all through your body.

After you are connected and grounded in this way, spend at least 20 to 30 minutes drinking in the purple and gold energies, allowing your body to be bathed in these healing frequencies.

Whatever technique you use to approach earthing, this powerful meditation tool and its healing benefits can be found at your fingertips — and felt in your toes!

For an in-depth look at more tips and tricks on curbing stress and anxiety, read Jean's min-e-book™, *Pants Down: How The Trousers-To-Toes Chakras Can Keep You Turned On, Tuned In, And Toned Up*, available through Absolute Love Publishing. Jean also is the author of *Atlantis Writhing* and an acupuncturist. Visit Jean at jeanbrannon.com.

MICHELLE HASTIE

BUILD CONFIDENCE
Before You Lose Weight

Losing weight is a physical goal frequently tied to the emotional goal of having more confidence. People often see confidence as something they *will* have once they are thinner, stronger, or better. It seems logical right? Shed pounds, get leaner, and the mirror will reflect a body that is worthy of confidence.

But in reality, that line of thought isn't logical. Instead, it's a lie we tell ourselves. The truth is our level of confidence has nothing to do with our weight.

Understandably, when we first lose weight, we may feel an initial boost of confidence along with the excitement of meeting our goal. Finally weighing less can feel like a major transformation on the inside as well as on the outside. And for a period of time, that can be true. But those initial feelings don't last.

Before we lose the weight we think that once we lose X number of pounds, we will be comfortable with attention. That we won't mind people noticing us. That we will feel more attractive. We say things like, "When I lose weight, I will be more confident to work out in public. When I have more endurance, I will join a group fitness class. When I'm leaner, I will do X, Y, and Z."

However, most people, after that initial boost of confidence wears off, find they are left with the original insecurities that fueled their desire to change their bodies in the first place.

If I were thinner, I would be accepted more ...
If I didn't have big thighs, I would be loved more ...

> *Confidence is an inside job. Changing the outside may grant us momentary relief from our insecurities, but the only true solution to gaining more confidence and defeating insecurities for good is to deal with our internal vulnerabilities. That means upgrading our emotional fitness alongside our physical fitness.*

I am so embarrassed by my waistline ...
What if people reject me or don't like me?
What if they think I look bad?

While we may receive a temporary reprieve from these thoughts with weight loss, these thoughts don't disappear along with the pounds on the scale. And so regardless of how in shape we become, we still are left to deal with our insecurities.

So what *do* we do about these insecurities if they aren't tied to how fit (or not) we are? We use the four C's to gain true confidence — whatever our shape, whatever our weight, whatever our mindset. But first, we must recognize two essential truths:

First, confidence is an inside job. Changing the outside may grant us momentary relief from our insecurities, but the only true solution to gaining more confidence and defeating insecurities for good is to deal with our internal vulnerabilities. That means upgrading our emotional fitness alongside our physical fitness. However, just as getting back into physical shape can be a challenge, so too can looking at the hurts and pains we have collected over the years and finding ways to heal them and let them go.

Second, we don't have to change our bodies to feel confident in them. Confidence can be built in any area of our lives so acknowledging success in anything we do can lead to greater confidence in our physical selves. For example: We are good at X, Y, and Z, whether or not we are thin. We are kind or supportive or funny or smart, whether or not we are thin.

Building Confidence by Stepping through the Four C's:

STEP ONE: COURAGE.

Before we can build confidence, we need to have the courage to go after something we don't feel confident enough to get. It takes courage to step out of our comfort zone and venture into new territory because there's safety in sameness — whether that's in how we act, what we do, or who we are. Even when we don't like what's familiar, there isn't any perceived risk in sticking to it. Striving for something new is risky and taking that risk gets us one step closer to true confidence.

STEP TWO: COMMITMENT.

Whether we're committing to running a mile, eating mindfully, learning how to play the guitar, or increasing our income, we need to be committed to achieving our goal. We don't yet have the steadfast confidence necessary to stay motivated to venture across new territory so we must depend on our commitment to the task at hand to pull us through and push us into the third step.

STEP THREE: CAPABILITY.

With courage and commitment, we start to pick up momentum. We become more capable in an area

It takes courage to step out of our comfort zone and venture into new territory because there's safety in sameness — whether that's in how we act, what we do, or who we are.

> With continual practice, we see it is *impossible* not to increase our capabilities in whatever area we've chosen to pursue.

where we were previously unskilled. For example, if we decided to commit to being a runner, we might find ourselves able to run a little further or faster at this point. If we committed to eating more mindfully, we might find it a little easier to eat more slowly and with more presence. With continual practice, we see it is *impossible* not to increase our capabilities in whatever area we've chosen to pursue. And that realization leads us to step four.

STEP FOUR: **CONFIDENCE.**

When we stay committed, continue to show up with courage, and allow our capabilities to continually increase, true confidence is the inevitable outcome. Unconvinced? Think about your first day at your current job compared to now or the first time you drove a car. You are miles away today from those early days simply by virtue of experience.

Let's consider a real life example:

Let's say you have always wanted to take Zumba, but you've felt uncoordinated and foolish when you've tried to dance or learn choreography. Cour-

age is showing up to that first class knowing you will feel uncomfortable. Knowing that you may be the "worst" one in the class. That you likely will have feelings you don't like.

Commitment is continuing to show up to that Zumba class despite knowing that it's going to be hard for a while and you may feel silly. It's going every week even though you may worry everyone is watching you make mistakes. And it's that commitment to showing up and doing the work that will help you move toward becoming a more confident dancer.

After continuing to take Zumba for a while, you notice you are a little more coordinated than when you first started. You still feel uncomfortable, but you notice improvement. Your capabilities are increasing.

With continuous practice, you eventually become a more confident Zumba student. You are able to pick up the moves quickly and dance to the songs smoothly. This makes you feel even more confident so you take on new songs as you start to remember the steps to songs you've done before, which enables you to look better when you dance. Eventually, you become a truly confident dancer.

While we discussed Zumba and dancing in this example, the four steps to true confidence can be utilized in any area of our lives. Confidence appears when we have the courage to show up and when we have the commitment to stick with it. And, as we build our skills through practice, our capabilities increase and our confidence soars.

Try this:

Instead of making decisions based on a goal of weight loss, focus on increasing your confidence. This creates a more accurate identity so you can focus on who you really are. If you are feeling insecure or inferior about one thing, brainstorm ways to increase your confidence in other things. Start showing yourself that you are courageous, committed, and capable.

As a bonus, the more we become who we really are, the more opportunities we give the body to release what isn't serving us — including any excess weight. It's a win-win!

Michelle Hastie has expertise in personal training, food psychology, neuro-linguistic programming, and yoga. She is the author of *The Weight Loss Shift: Be More, Weigh Less*, *The Chakra Secret: What Your Body Is Telling You*, and *Have Your Cake and Be Happy, Too: A Joyful Approach to Weight Loss* and is a *Women Will Save the World* contributor. Visit www.totalbodyhealthsolutions.com.

HEART CHAKRA RECIPE

by Chef Maria Schonder

Greens rule when it comes to your heart chakra. Salads, kale smoothies, green grapes, all these lift up your love center. You can support your heart simply by adding a side of green veggies to every meal! For an added bonus, turn to this recipe – one of my favorites! It is warm, nourishing, and delicious. Feel free to make any adaptations you wish. If you don't have collard greens or kale, add Swiss chard or dandelion greens or whatever else you have. Play around with it, and create your own signature soup!

Detox Mug o' Love Soup

4 servings

INGREDIENTS

4 cups broth of choice (preferably homemade)
1 bunch broccoli, stems peeled, chopped
1 bunch collard greens or kale, tough stems removed
2 carrots, chopped
1 lemon, juiced
Salt to taste

DIRECTIONS

Heat broth in a large pot.
Add broccoli and carrots. Simmer for 5 minutes.
Add collards or kale and simmer for 10 additional minutes.
Add vegetables and broth to a blender in batches. Puree until smooth.
Return to pot, and season with lemon juice and salt to taste.

From Michelle Hastie's
*The Chakra Secret: What
Your Body Is Telling You,* a
min-e-book™

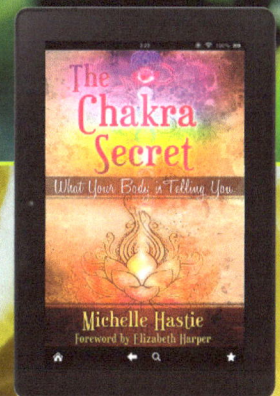

The Chakra Secret
What Your Body is Telling You
Michelle Hastie
Foreword by Elizabeth Harper

I See You

Denise Thompson

Recently I was standing in line at my local grocery store. It was a busy day, and people were acting a little restless and rushed, ready to complete their shopping and be on their way. Cutting through the noise was a repeated "I see you" coming from the crowd, along with some unusual sounds.

I turned to see a young man standing behind me, directing these words and sounds to all those around him and anyone who would look his way. One person, not understanding the unusual sounds and statement, looked behind with a scowl. Other people ignored him and simply looked away. Some just kept their faces neutral.

But this young man was persistent.

I turned around to look at this family, intending to offer a smile and eye contact, and perhaps even a shared message of understanding.

Again, I heard the boy say, "I see you" to no response. It was then that it clicked.

I turned around, looked directly at him and said, "I see YOU." He gave me a radiant smile and happily turned back to his family. As I paid for my groceries, I heard someone in his family say, "Is that what you were looking for?"

As I left the store, I started thinking. Isn't that what we all are looking for? To be seen and to be heard?

It was a small experience, but it made a deep impact on me. It made me question what I choose to see and what I choose to ignore, who I choose to acknowledge and who I choose to keep separate. In an important way, I saw myself in that young man. I recognized the need we all have to be seen – and I also remembered the joy I feel when I encounter someone who takes a moment to say, "I see you."

LAW OF
POLARITY

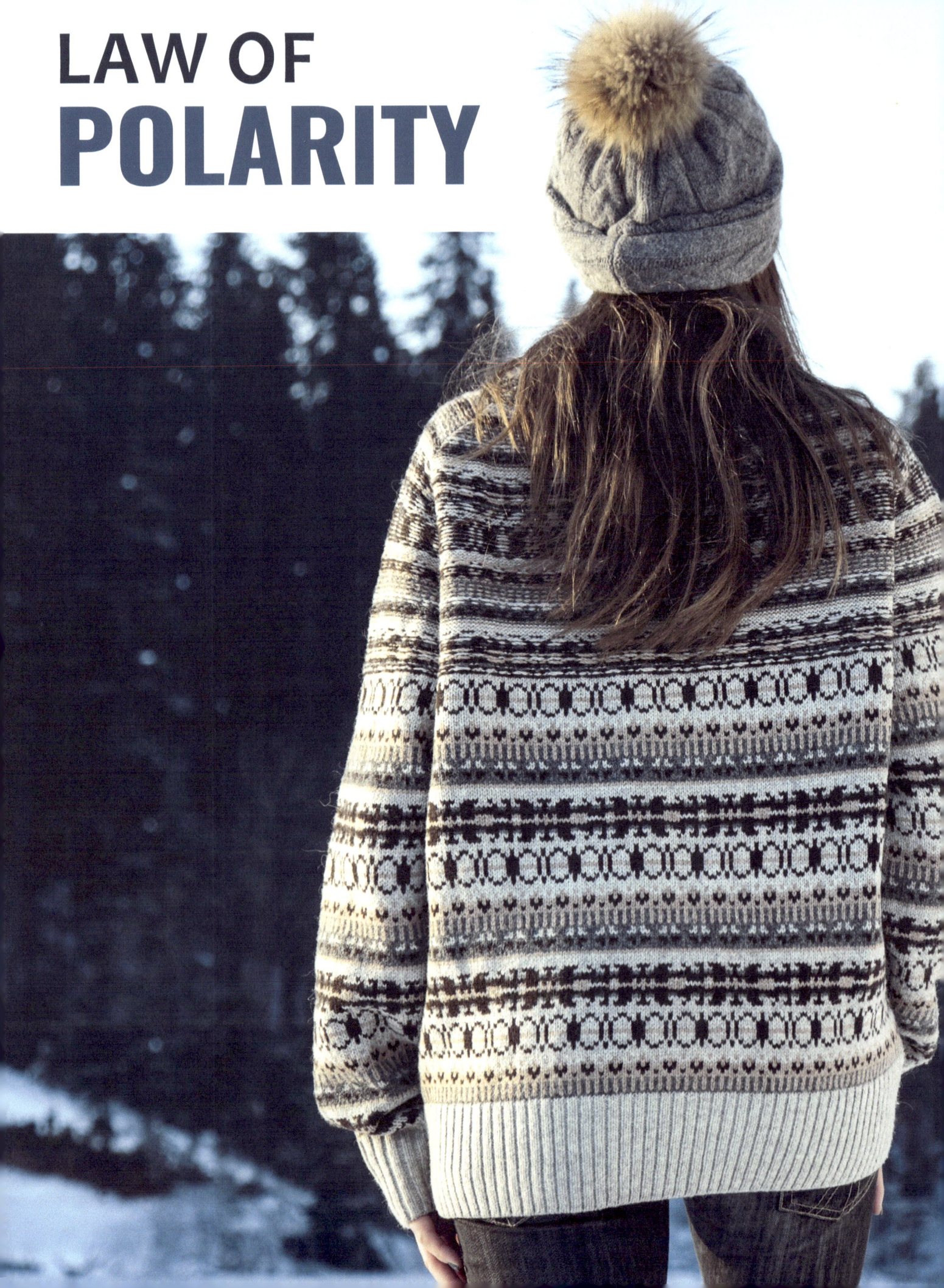

Caroline A. Shearer

The Universal Law of Polarity says that everything has an equal and exact opposite and that opposites are on the same continuum. For example, financial abundance and financial lack would be opposites on the same continuum.

What this means is, regardless of what you consider your level of "success" at manifesting, you are on the continuum, and creating the result you want is just a matter of switching the polarity of your intention.

Using the example of financial abundance and financial lack, there are extremes on both of those sides: extreme abundance and extreme lack. Likely, you are somewhere in the middle, with any shift to the "positive" side of the scale feeling like a win.

To achieve this, you'd have to look first at your primary motivations for money and your thought patterns about having money. You also might compare how your motivations and thought patterns conflict or are in harmony. For example, perhaps your motivation to create money involves you being able to do lots of wonderful things that will make life better for yourself and others. But perhaps your thought patterns tell you that you are not successful enough to ever create that kind of, well, success. The same would be true of love or health or anything else you'd like to manifest. And just like the currents of a battery, if your thoughts and motivations are working against each other, they are in effect canceling each other out.

That leaves two potential actions for you to take. You can switch your thoughts and motivations to their opposite, if needed. You also can look at how those energies might be conflicting and how you can create instead a positive, one-directional flow.

Try this for a good visual: take out a piece of paper and draw a scale with left negative and right positive. Write down your thoughts and motivations about the subject in the places they would appear on a scale. Where does your motivation fall and where do your overall thoughts fall?

To use the Law of Polarity, imagine what the thoughts or motivations on the left side would be if you switched them to the opposite side. What nudge (or leap) could you make by switching that thought or motivation to its positive? And what conflicting energies could you release by making sure your motivations and thoughts are in harmony?

This activity alone can help you shift your polarity to a positive flow.

But in addition to this deeper work, there are also practical, everyday ways you can incorporate the Law of Polarity. If you're feeling sad, you could choose to wallow. Or, you could look to the opposite of sad, and do something that brings you joy, whether that is watching a funny movie or playing with a cat. If you're feeling mad, instead of lashing out, you can use the energy of that continuum to get something done or have a great workout.

Recognizing that our emotions and thoughts aren't separate, that they are indeed part of a continuum, is an important tool in creating a high-vibration life and one that can help us create a mental connection that shifts the power of our intentions in a magnetic way. Are you ready for a positive charge?

CONSCIOUS FINANCE

Having ample money is powerful because it matches the power of your soul. Being abundant provides a vibration that matches your soul and allows it to serve its greater purpose in this life without hindrance.

Being poor diminishes your soul, the brightness and the beauty of it. Being poor is a trick of the ego to slow you down. It also can feed your ego with feelings of self-righteousness or martyrdom.

When we are children we grow from whatever experiences we have in relation to our parents' wealth or poverty, but once we are in charge of our own financial reality, it is not noble to accept poverty. It is noble to accept that we are meant for wealth.

It is a misconception to believe we have to have money problems to learn more about money. We can learn more about abundance by having it, in the same way that we learn more about love by experiencing it.

Based on *Raise Your Financial Vibration* by Caroline A. Shearer

The wealth within you, your essence, is your kingdom.
- Rumi

It is not "higher" to be poor, for it often takes money to accomplish your life's work.
- *Creating Money: Attracting Abundance* by Sanaya Roman

ENERGY
SPEAKS

Messages from Spirit on
LIVING, LOVING,
and AWAKENING

LEE HARRIS

Foreword by Regina Meredith

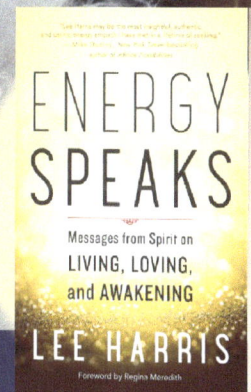

"The Universe is a little like a bank with branch locations all over the place, and you are constantly investing your love here, there, and everywhere. It multiplies your love and offers it back to you all of the time through other routes — other faces, other events, other experiences. If you are focused on receiving only in certain areas and from certain people, especially those that are often the recipients of your giving, you might miss the person knocking on your front door. You might refuse them at first because you have given this stranger nothing, and you do not even recognize who he or she is. Yet no one has a problem with Santa, oddly enough, even though no one has met him!

As a child, you quite loved this idea of a man who has never met you, who comes around and gives you a bunch of presents. He does this every year, for free, for you. Children have no problem receiving in that way.

Santa is the Universe. Father Christmas is the Universe. And the Universe wants to give to you."

~ *Energy Speaks* by Lee Harris

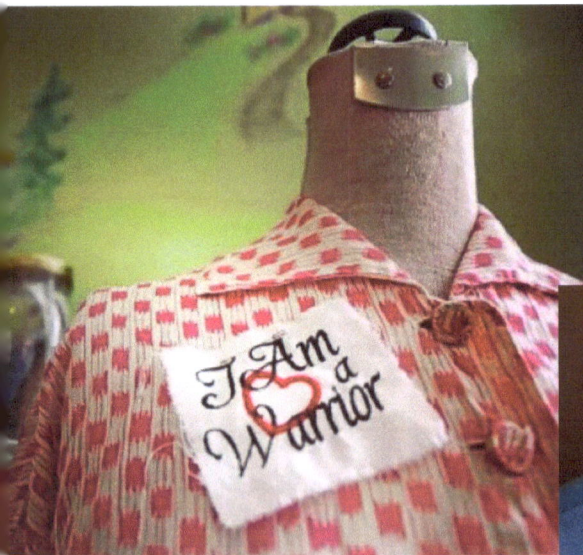

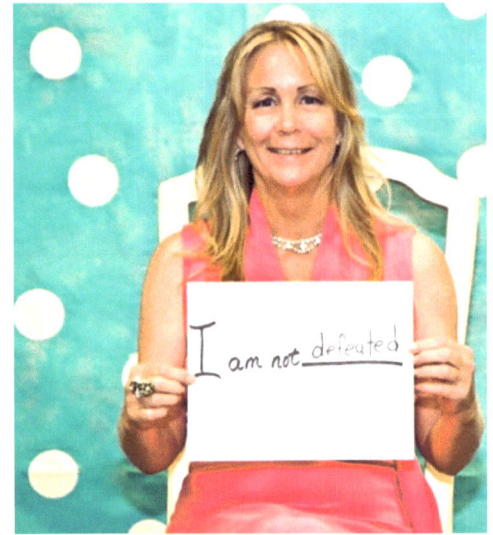

Respond to negative thoughts as you would to small children who do not know any better; simply smile and show them a better way to be.
- *Creating Money: Attracting Abundance* by Sanaya Roman

I am Wise Affirmations

from *Women Will Save the World*

I exercise discernment in my choices.

I honor the wisdom I possess at every age and stage of my life and through all challenges and all situations.

I actively free myself from external noise, allowing my inner wisdom to shine.

I make the best decisions I am capable of at the time and allow myself to make different decisions later.

I share my wisdom with those who are ready to hear it, and I am gracious with those who are not.

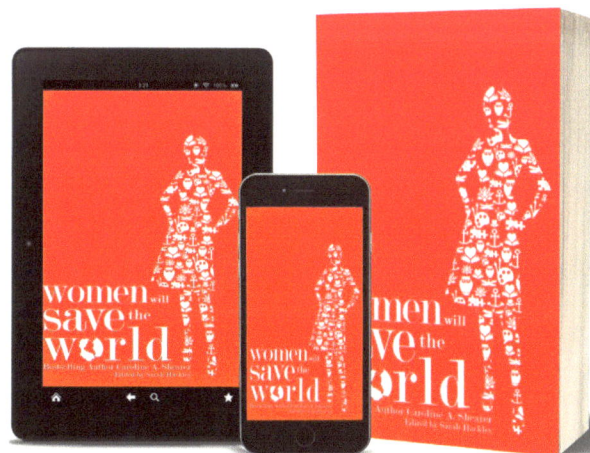

ATTENTION, LIBRARY LOVERS!

Did you know you can request that any of the Absolute Love Publishing books be purchased by your local library? For most library systems, it's as easy as filling out a short online form. Contact your library today to request our books, and help yourself and other patrons enjoy them for years to come!

The "I am Grateful for..." ring features two surfaces that move independently, allowing you to spin the ring each time you feel grateful. This dynamic tool creates a positive trigger in the brain, increasing positive thinking and a feeling of well-being. **Buy one today at www.gratefulring.com.**

DEAD END DATE

A woman's journey to teach the world about love, one mystery and personal hang-up at a time

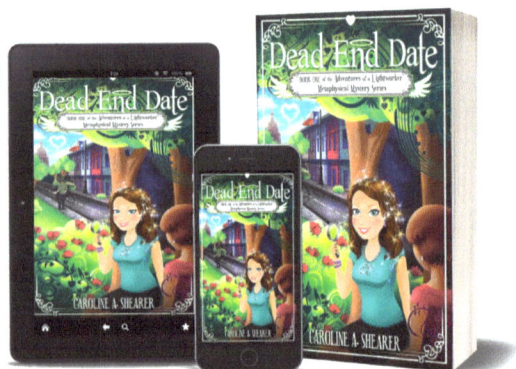

WWW.ABSOLUTELOVEPUBLISHING.COM/SHOP

BOOK CLUBS & MORE

Are you in a book club? Absolute Love Publishing offers discounts for bulk purchases, including for book clubs and organizations. We also offer incentive bonuses, such as online Q&A's with the author with a minimum purchase.

Visit our online store to see what options are publicly available, and/or email us for more information on how you can qualify for a discount or a bonus.

Store: www.absolutelovepublishing.com/shop
Email: publisher@absolutelovepublishing.com

LOVE ALOVEDLIFE?

Be sure to read every edition of this evergreen publication! Check our store, and sign up for our emails to catch each issue!

MOM LIFE: Perfection Pending

"Extraordinary and highly recommended"
"A delightful, identifiable, and entertaining read from cover to cover"
- *Midwest Book Review*

www.absolutelovepublishing.com/shop

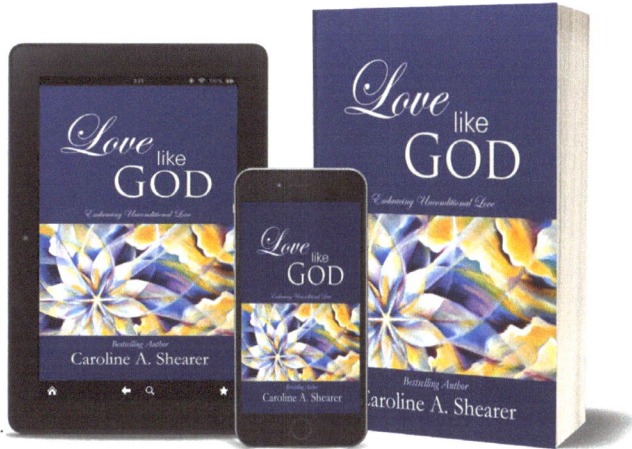

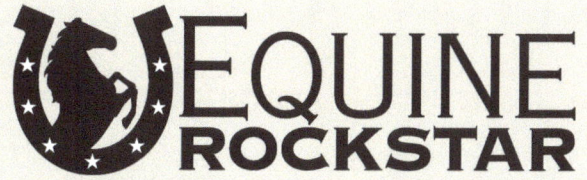

Maybe you are searching among the branches, for what only appears in the roots.
- Rumi

ATTENTION, TEACHERS & SCHOOLS!

What better way to promote a love of reading and writing than to host an author at your school? The Absolute Love Publishing authors are available for both in-person and Skype visits, and we can work with you to create the best outcome for your students. Contact ambassador@absolutelovepublishing.com today!

MIDDLE GRADE BOOKS

YOUNG ADULT BOOKS

Five-Minute Essential Oils

Essential oils and aromatic tinctures have been used around the world for thousands of years for general health and wellness, as well as to heal the wounded and ill.

Making the time to meditate for even five minutes daily while inhaling an essential oil (or blend of oils) speaks directly to your brain through the inhalation process to calm, energize, or enhance how you are feeling.

Blends of single or multiple scents can create a soothing atmosphere for relaxation, which is a key factor in meditation. Depending on the scents you choose, oils can promote grounding, balance, health, sensuality, peace, clarity, energy, or happiness.

Try these common essentials oils alone or together to combine a pleasing aroma to set the mood and feed your senses. Use them by adding a few drops of each essential oil to your diffuser or carrier oil. Adjust oil amount to less or more based on your preferences.

Lavender - floral, calming
Frankincense - woodsy, sweet
Peppermint - cool, invigorating
Cedarwood - woodsy, grounding
Rose Geranium - floral, rosy
Orange - citrus, energizing
Vetiver - calming, earthy
Bergmot - mild, citrusy
Rosemary - evergreen, clean
Sandalwood - spicy, woodsy, sweet

Here are some examples of how you can create certain moods:

Bedtime calm and relaxation: lavender
Energy and clarity: grapefruit, lime, and rosemary
Sensuality and romance: sandalwood, rose geranium, and bergamot
Purification and energy: peppermint

A wise man ought to realize that health is his mostvaluablepossession.
- Hippocrates

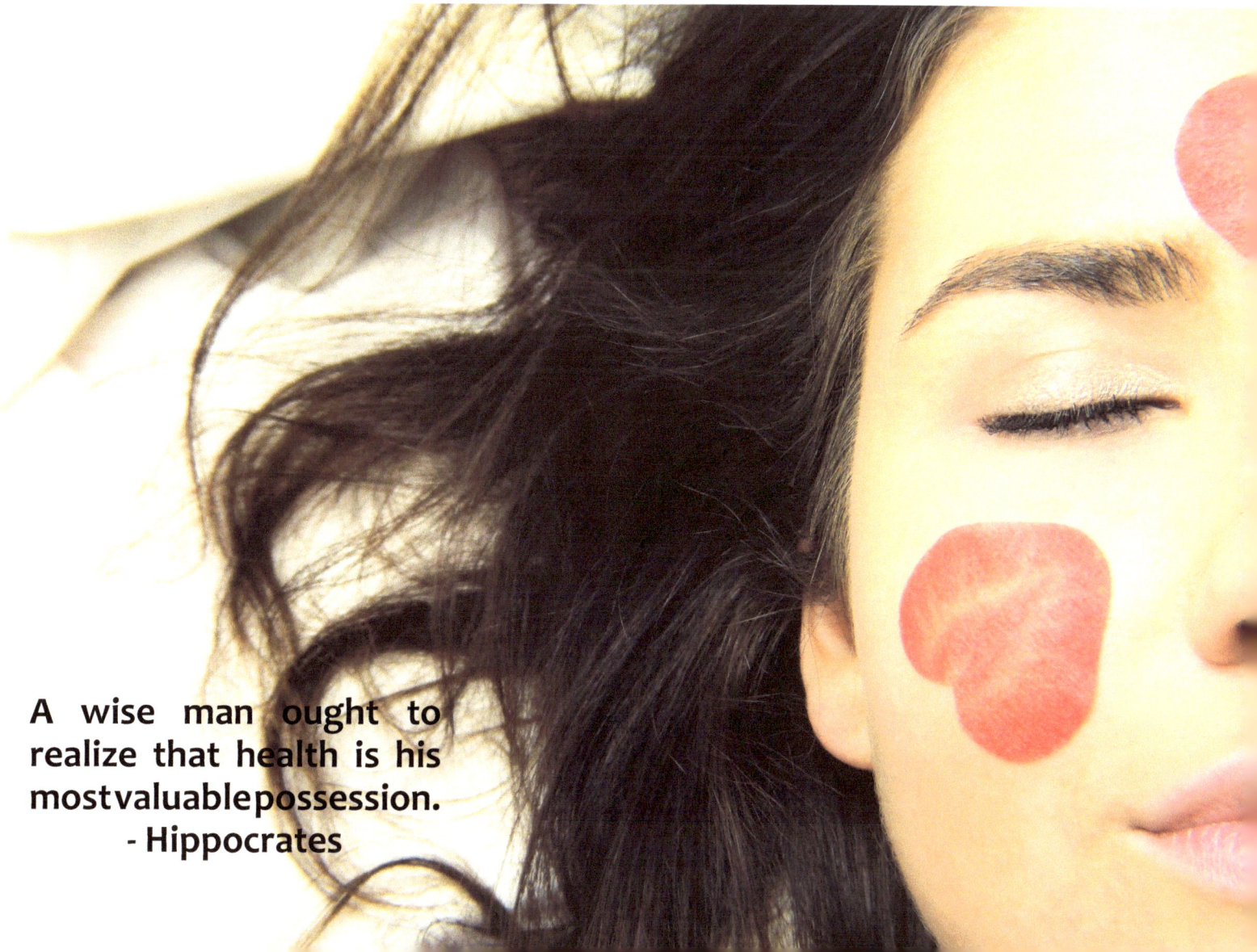

You can rise above mass consciousness and experience divine consciousness instead.

~ Personal Power through Awareness by Sanaya Roman

www.ingramcontent.com/pod-product-compliance
Lightning Source LLC
Chambersburg PA
CBHW042006080426
42733CB00003B/20

9 780999 577387